# INSTITUTIONS AT PLAY

## FUSION AND FISSION OF EUROPEAN LAW

*"Comparative Legal Studies"*

Scientific Series Directed by
ANTONELLO MIRANDA

Antonello Miranda

# INSTITUTIONS AT PLAY

## FUSION AND FISSION OF EUROPEAN LAW

L'Harmattan Italia
via Degli Artisti 15
10124 Torino

L'Harmattan
5-7 rue de l'École Polytechnique
75005 Paris

ISBN (Italia) : 978-88-7892-530-4

ISBN (France) : 978-2-336-56917-8

harmattan.italia@gmail.com / www.editions-harmattan.fr

# CONTENTS

*For my second best life*

# FOREWORD

CARL STYCHIN

*Director of the Institute of Advanced Legal Studies - London University*

Could there be a more opportune moment to pause and reflect on the key historical cases in the law of the European Union and the political and historical context which surrounded them? I write this as someone who has had their European citizenship rights removed from them; who has been subjected to interminable, intellectually bereft arguments about 'sovereignty' in the British media; and who now watches with horror at the rise of extreme nationalism on the European continent leading to invasion and war. In this moment of existential crisis for Europe, pr. Antonello Miranda offers us a forensic re-examination of some of the founding moments in the story of European Union law.

In so doing, pr. Antonello Miranda also provides a unique, illuminating insight into comparative legal systems. He excavates the challenges which surrounded the arrival of common law judges within a Court which had been built upon the foundations of the civilian system.

This is a fascinating tale which particularly should be read by those who continue to be enamoured by nineteenth century views of the sovereign Nation State. However, for me, as a citizen of the United Kingdom, it is inevitably a poignant story in the current political climate.

The irony, as pr. Miranda carefully demonstrates, is that judges from the United Kingdom Courts have had a very substantial role in shaping how the relationship between the

European Union and the Member States is today understood.

This careful, interdisciplinary analysis should be widely read in order to broaden our understanding of the supranational context of the European Union. Finally, my hope is that it might raise our collective understanding of the legal and political challenges which we face today.

# PREFACE

MASHA ANTOKOLSKAIA

*Full Professor of Private and Family Law at the Vrije University of Amsterdam, President of the International Society of Family Law*

*A concise, but masterly performed analysis*

This relatively short book is in many ways a breakthrough, as Antonello Miranda is one of the few pro-European scholars, who dare to openly deal with things we always wanted to know about the EU but were afraid to ask. One of the 'damned questions' he addresses is the nature of the European legal order and the matter of supremacy of European law and limitation of the sovereignty of the Member States. In our increasingly polarized world, critical assessment of these matters was long left to the Eurosceptics, while pro-European scholars were merely 'defending' those crucial concepts from the attacks of adversaries. That is unfortunate, as earlier critical attention by the pro-European camp to these 'damned questions', might have prevented Brexit and still can save us a lot of misery with rebelling Eastern European countries.

Antonello Miranda's profound understanding of history and logic of both the common law and civil law legal mentality and appreciation of legal sources and their inter-relation, allows him to get down to the nitty-gritty of the matter. He masterly compares the civil law paradigm of hierarchy of legal sources, based on the fusion and 'one-or-the-other' perception, which logically leads to the construct supremacy of EU law with the common law paradigm of fission and 'one-next-to-the-other' perception, which allows for the co-existence of equal entities with divided competences.

A concise, but masterly performed analysis of the relevant principal ECJ cases provides a convincing empirical basis for his theoretical standpoint.

The whole endeavour appears to be a prelude and calls for more. Comparing the correlation of European and national law with that of common law and equity provides very promising perspectives well beyond the blunt perception of such a correlation merely in terms of supremacy and subordination. Any other possible helpful comparisons lie much further back in history. One may, however, think of the correlation between Roman civil law and Praetorian law; or the uniform Canon (Family) law of the Catholic Church and the (family) law of the national States from 11$^{th}$ to 16$^{th}$ century.

This concise book makes the reader wonder if some things in the EU legal order have evolved from something we all agreed to, into something quite different. Or in the words of Antonello Miranda, who is a great connoisseur of cocktails, have we not started drinking a Negroni, which we had ordered, and ended up drinking a Bellini, which, while tasting delicious, was still something we had never ordered. If that is indeed the case, perhaps it is better to accept that, and try to do something constructive with it, rather than to keep trying to convince all the cocktail party guests that they are still drinking Negroni?

# PROLOGUE

OLEKSIY KRESIN

*Doctor of Legal Sciences, Professor, Associated Member of International Academy of Comparative Law, Head of Comparative Jurisprudence Centre "Volodymyr Koretskyi Institute of State and Law" (National Academy of Sciences of Ukraine), Visiting Fellow (Department of Political Science - University of Palermo)*

*A concise book with a profound purport*

The book by pr. Antonello Miranda is interesting reading for a comparative lawyer. For on materials of EU law and Member States law(s) interaction he raises and develops the core questions of national legal systems survival and transformation, the very nature of the integrated legal order. So, fusion or fission of European law, hierarchy or delegation?

As a starting point the author takes the idea of the sovereign, comprehensive and even total national legal order we inherited from the era of nationalism, mass codifications and Constitutions creation in Continental Europe two centuries ago, and the same Continental idea of the same age of the systematic nature of a national legal order with a clear hierarchy of the sources of law being the skeleton of the system and a key element of Civil law mentality.

Antonello Miranda compares these ideas and presumptions with common law approaches, and substantial and methodological insights taken from political science(s), history, biographical studies, linguistics, physics etc. One of the keys here is the author's hypothesis of the long-lasting influence of the European Court of Justice judges with a common law background on interpretation and development of EU law. This, in the author' opinion, provides for the possibility to view some existential for EU law issues according to the common law approach, which is now largely neglected both in European law and comparative law studies.

For Antonello Miranda, European law should be viewed through the lens of EU competences in interaction with Member States competences rather than that of a (semi-)comprehensive legal system. In this vision the issue of hierarchy and subordination is disappearing and coexistence is becoming the focus.

The author, developing some predecessors' ideas, claims that EU law is not so much a substantive legal order, but rather a mechanism of delegated law-making and judicature, working in the name of all Member States and within limited competences. While the EU obtained legal personality with the will of Member States it lacks such a principal characteristic as "the ability to act in all matters not specifically excluded".

The common law approach, according to Antonello Miranda, may be viewed twofold. He stresses the absence of an idea of strong hierarchy of sources of law in common law. This means, first of all, that no supremacy of EU law over a Member State law exists, but just a full or partial transfer of certain powers controlled by every Member State. Secondly, it means that the law of Member States and the EU law coexist in a single space as, to some extent, equal sources of law in a single legal order the same as classical common law and the law of Equity. According to the author, EU law could be considered to be special compared to State law in general, and the latter could be disapplied (without denying or questioning its validity) by the former in certain matters and limits. The scheme here, in the author's vision, is not a vertical line with a top to down vector or even vice versa, not a loop, not the chemical fusion, but the chain reaction of their interaction and mutual modification – fission, "creating new entities and developing new energies destined to meet again".

An additional approach and some theses accompany these ideas. The approach providing quite a widespread private law vision of public law – as being private in essence (for being a law at all), but influenced by politics. The first thesis is that EU law and the law(s) of Member States could be viewed as "conflicting and coexisting jurisdictions", and concrete norms of different origin could be viewed as conflicting or colliding according to international private law, taking "people's and parties' autonomy" as a principle. The second, quite hidden one, is the author's scepticism about international (public) law.

In this worldview EU law disappears as a separate phenomenon: EU simply appears as a coordination mechanism, lawmaking and judicial body built in national legal systems; EU law is just an integral part of national law(s). EU legal acts in certain areas may be superior or, rather, of preference, priority, prevalence, or precedence (disapplying, or setting-aside certain norms created by a State itself), but they still have to be viewed as norms, the creation of which was merely delegated (or provided as the power of attorney in private law "to legally act in its own name and on its own behalf") by a State to other inter-State bodies, "clearly within a definite scope and always limited and subsidiary in nature", and this does not entail any superiority of EU law as a whole: "an intrinsic 'validity' of domestic law which does not stop being recognized outside of the specific field covered by community norms". Legal acts, created by inter-State bodies according to inter-State treaties, are limiting to some extent the freedom of national law-creating and law-enforcing bodies, but just as a consequence of the decision to delegate some functions by the State in exercising its power, and so the State's sovereignty in the legal sphere is in no way limited.

The State and State law in Antonello Miranda's book, in my opinion, no longer refer to the Modern total and absolute sovereignty model. But they are not post-modern either, they preserve their institutional autonomy. The (seeming) autochthonism giving way to inner pluralism of equal legal formants (I have taken this term from the unforgettable Italian scholar Rodolfo Sacco) of diverse origin. But the hierarchical structure of sources of law is to some extent giving way to the conflict-of-law rules thus transforming the model while securing the essence of the very system city of the national legal system.

However, I believe some contradiction with these ideas lies in the text itself. The State (dominus) cannot "in self-defence ignore nor revoke the conferred power, therefore accepting all consequences of the delegate's conduct in advance". The delegate / attorney (EU with its law) becoming more and more active in its actions and the conferred power leading to the creation of the sphere of autonomy of its law, more and more extensively understood, where the primacy of the delegate's norms over that independently created by a State (and also its lawyers and society) is obvious. Of course, this is not overall hierarchy between legal systems, but provides for a supremacy in certain spheres. And the delegate acquired its own supranational executive and judicial institutions to protect its sphere of autonomy. It is important that the delegate represents the interest of not just one, but a number of clients (States), and its acts and decisions thus in some matters mirror the compromise between them, interests of a majority of them, members of their families' (people's) demands, and its own interest (interests of the growing European bureaucracy) – thus frequently distorting or simply ignoring the will of a particular client. The development of the EU (delegate) legal order, of course, to some extent may be seen as the fission of Member States national legal systems in certain spheres and their completion in other (new) ones while generating new energy. But the reduction of the ever more autonomous legal order to a sum of its norms and their implementation in national legal orders seems to me as being partial truth.

But this contradiction is not a shortcoming of Antonello Miranda's book. It is a mirror of the general uncertainty of the theory and methodology of comparative law. One of the main points is an antinomy between modern and post-modern reasoning. While modern reasoning presupposes in one or another way the inviolability, systemicity, and totality of the national legal system thus in fact leaving no geographical or normative space for other types of legal orders, post-modern reasoning points to the legal pluralism inside, among, and in spite of national law. The former construction lacks the realistic vision, and the latter deconstruction lacks the ordered and structured world picture.

The foundations of post-postmodernism in comparative law (here I refer to the works of prominent Ukrainian comparatists Oleksandr Tykhomyrov and Oleksandr

Tkachenko) have to synthetize philosophical and theoretical bases of both modernism and post-modernism providing for the measured and ordered plurality inside, among and in parallel with national law. And this order cannot be a monopoly in the hands of one type of legal system and cannot presuppose the overall supremacy of one type of legal system, it should rest on the effects of inter-system ties and interactions and the dynamic nature of legal transformations. Thus, this should be, maybe, an ordered web (the quite forgotten idea of British scholar Sir Julian Sorell Huxley). But all these searches are on the way and no scholar can pretend he/she already proposed philosophical and theoretical bases able to absorb and transcend modernism and post-modernism both as living practices and worldviews.

So, what does Italian pr. Antonello Miranda propose if his ideas are to be seen in this context? He is constructing a new post-postmodernist model incorporating national law and integrated law in a single, ordered pluralist space, operated with a horizontal coordination and interaction conflict-of-law mechanism, to explain the transformations of legal orders. A concise book with a profound purport.

# 1. INTRODUCTION

The title and the subject of this study need clarification, more precisely an explanation of the highly personal reasons that led to this choice[1]. Indeed, in all these years of lectures and research, I had often promised myself to put something down on paper on this subject. Yet, because of the almost unanimous and numerous voices of jurists (and others) on the SUPREMACY of European law and limitations to the sovereignty of Member States, I gave up. I gave up because it seemed to me to be a topic relating to another "scientific field" somehow far removed from my studies, and I believed that no one, not even I, would ever forgive that intrusion[2]. Today, however, with the so-called crisis of multilateralism, the increasingly cumbersome presence of new powers and new international balances, the evident crisis of the European Union (not only attributable to Brexit) and the 'nationalist' reaction of the constitutional Courts of some Member States, I have the opportunity to freely put into words some reflections that I could not have done some time ago.

I immediately wish to reassure my "twenty-five readers"[3] that, despite what is being said these days, and despite the title of this book, my approach is far from Eurosceptic and pro-British, although – I must admit – I have always appreciated the British pragmatic approach to the EU, its duties and related roles[4]. However, having had the good fortune to follow the development and growth of the Union and the work of the Court of Justice since my law school university years, I have never given up the doubt that the *Trimurti* of the Community and its reincarnations were something completely different from whatever kind of "international organisation" was then known, and any other kind of "superstate" or "federal State". In other words, even though as a young liberal I always felt a pull towards the United States of Europe, as a young jurist I could not fully convince myself of any justification or the fundamental reasons for this undesirable and logically unjustified subordination of a Member State to the European Community.

There were too many ambiguities and logical leaps in the texts of those years (which are still read as a classic *path dependency*), and perhaps too much collusion – even unintentional – between the jurists sent to Brussels, Luxembourg or Strasbourg, which could never have killed the goose that laid the golden eggs[5]. To put it more simply, it was a doctrinal approach, highly successful with both the public and the critics, based on the perspective lines and the use of categories typical of the scientific disciplines of "institutional legal-political" and international law, at the time and then for a long time, considerably "Europeanist". In my opinion, however, doubts arose above all about the problem of the 'transfer and limitation of powers' by the Member State and the reference to article 11 of the Italian Constitution[6] as an element justifying the supremacy of Community law.

Moreover, as I was about to defend my master's thesis at the time, I ended up discussing the fascinating Simmenthal case, which had been freshly published at the time[7]. As an aspiring comparatist, that judgment caught my attention, not only because of the well-known issue of the disapplication of domestic law in favour of what was then called European Community law (and is now known as EU law), but also because that decision – unlike the earlier "Van Gend en Loos", "Costa *v* Enel" and "Internationale Handelsgesellschaft" judgements – was handed down after the accession of the United Kingdom to the EEC[8], and consequently with an unprecedented and peculiar composition of the Court of Justice that included judges and general attorneys of common law, such as Jean-Pierre F. E. Warner, Andreas O'Keefe and, above all, Alexander J. Mackenzie Stuart, later given the title of Baron Mackenzie Stuart of Dean.

Personally, I consider the composition of the Courts and, this Court in particular (and constitutional and supreme Courts in general[9]) to be an extremely important peculiarity. Although it is a trivial rule that the entire "collegium" makes the decision, this body is composed of human beings. In turn, human beings inevitably include their socio-cultural backgrounds and political views in their decisions[10], since not everyone is Saint Thomas Beckett.

We must admit that in the context of constitutional Courts as well as supreme Courts, the "profile" of the judges, as well as their experience, play an important role as the men and women carry personal ideas with them as demonstrated by the care taken in establishing the US Supreme Court control system, tailored to reduce the risk of an excessively "strong" and "evident" political burden to a minimum[11] or the complex method adopted to "compose" the group of jurors, from the Jury pool to the Jury box, in the USA system[12].

Moreover, Law cannot be likened to biology (I know this is a trivial statement almost like saying things are not what they used to be…) and despite the fact that jurists are scientists like others, they cannot approach their science like biologists and physicists do, by studying and observing a phenomenon without DECIDING which of virus A and virus B is right. If you decide, you cannot do it entirely aseptically. Now, this is neither good nor bad, however when a jurist critically analyses a decision, in my opinion, he cannot avoid taking into consideration this "variable" too.

We are thus faced with a LATENT CHARACTERISING MARK of the legal system, which ends up influencing the generation and evolution of the law.

Although this is not the place to deal with this subject, it is appropriate, also to understand the method I followed in this analysis, to explain at least the terms of reference.

In fact, in this study I do not refer (only) to the theory of formants so widespread among Italian, European and American comparatists, or to the system of sources, but attempt to highlight how, in comparing the different legal systems and in evaluating the solutions adopted by them or their experiences, it is necessary, exactly as it is for the "hard sciences" when comparing two samples, to identify and highlight the constituent elements that, whether visible or hidden, determine the peculiarity of each of them, as though they were a sort of "DNA", or indelible and characterising marks, "tattoos" or particular scars.

In other words, I will consider the 'signs' in the sense of semeiotics, which characterise the individual systems and which allow us to understand and explain the underlying reasons for the differences and similarities and therefore to understand the systems themselves and the solutions adopted better and more precisely.

If, on the one hand, resorting to the theory of the sources of law only gives us a partial and static picture of the individual systems, on the other, not even the theory of formants seems to give us a complete and fully satisfactory picture of the "dynamics" of the systems compared.

The theory of legal formants (*i formanti,* masculine in Italian) and crypto-types – or hidden formants – as it is known, was formulated by Rodolfo Sacco[13] who argued that "living law contains many different elements, such as legal norms, scholars' formulations, judges' decisions and so on".

Following this line of thought and considering that formants are "everything that influences the formation of a legal system at a given time", it is argued that in every legal system one can find at least three "basic" formants, namely: the legal formant (everything that contributes to the production – and imposition – of a legal norm), the judicial formant (everything that contributes to the resolution of disputes) and the doctrinal formant (everything that concerns the interpretation and reconstruction of legal concepts). These elements influence each other and may vary in importance, value and weight from one system to another, leading a careful scholar to measure the actual scope of the individual formants to perceive with certainty, when comparing different systems, the actual extent of the norms studied.

Sacco mentioned that he formulated this theory while discussing with his brother who was working on his dissertation in phonetics. In this respect, however, the term "formants", if indeed borrowed as a concept from acoustic phonetics, should be declined into the feminine form "*la formante, le formanti*": i.e. 'each of the components of the acoustic spectrum that distinguish the different timbres of a vowel' as in the definition given in the Treccani dictionary.

I assume that the use of the masculine form by the creator of the theory is essentially due to the fact that he wanted to emphasise in this way that the concept is different (unless he wanted to use the term "formant" as in linguistics – but in this case the meaning is still different as in linguistics it serves "to indicate the linguistic element or affix that is added to the radical part of a word, forming a verbal or nominal theme").

In simpler terms, I believe that Sacco deduced that the sound of a vowel changes not only because of the physical conformation of the person generating the sound, but also because of the presence of elements such as the distance of the listener, the presence of elements of distortion (such as the walls of a room or the different composition of the places, etc.) and even the physical conformation of the listener. We all pronounce the letter "a" but the sound that is emitted differs according to the different factors that contribute to "forming" that sound as well as its final perception.

In this sense, while departing from the theory of phonetics, Sacco possibly meant to say that when looking at the "rules" declared in a given legal system, it was necessary to consider everything that could contribute to their formation and their real and effective scope, highlighting the reasons why in different legal systems, "declarations" of the same rules can sometimes correspond to different operational rules and/or vice versa.

However, while perusing the many texts and writings on comparative law in Italy, I noticed that almost all speak of formants using the term as a synonym for sources of law and some authors even use the terms indiscriminately; that formants and sources are two different things seems to me to be logical and evident; unfortunately, it does not seem to me that this very clear distinction is exactly clear and obvious to Scholars. I challenge anyone to find an Italian author who is able to explain exactly what the differences are with sources and what the "formants" actually consist of, apart from the usual generic references to the dynamic approach to comparative law and the function performed by "someone" who is "institutionally involved in the creative activity of law" or the "legal basis on which a legal system develops" or the "single elements or mechanisms that operate even before the normative production and that are in fact its profound cause": like saying, *obscurum per obscurius*, that the *"causa"* is the socio-economic function of the contract... or that there are no longer any half-seasons.

If, on the other hand, taking up the concept of the formants and considering that legal comparison is a science in itself and therefore subject to the "rules" of any scientific comparison, we were to consider the 'formants' as part of fundamental elements (I would say constitutional or, to avoid confusion, constitutive elements) without which there is no legal system, being precisely its DNA, and use the "science of signs" to identify them, I believe that the difference with the sources of law would be much clearer, and it would also be clearer to understand their function and role in the formation of the single legal system. But this is a discussion that takes us too far away and ends up trespassing into areas such as the difference between taxonomy and systemology on the one hand and systematics on the other.

Be that as it may, what I would like to highlight here is the "Italian-style" use of the comparative method, applied also to the analysis of "European Union law", which cannot be exactly understood in its nuances and complexity or in its fallout on the legal systems of the Member States if not, precisely, by approaching it dynamically and not purely exegetically or in terms of hierarchy of sources and supremacy. Which entails us to review the general approaches and even the idea we have of legal comparison. Indeed, in many countries there is an idea and consideration of comparative law anchored to rather rigid stereotypes dating back to the last century. The comparative law practised in Germany, and also widely used in English-speaking countries, often limits itself to observing the rules present in the various legal systems without, however, hardly ever going into the depths of the "real" explanation of any differences or similarities. Sometimes one looks at the "circulation of a model" or observes a hypothetical legal transplant but hardly ever grasps the reasons why the model has been successful (or not). Still worse when the "comparatist" simply reads foreign law without interpreting the socio-political and economic background that necessarily characterises it. On the contrary, as I was saying, European law has also gone beyond the international dimension to the transnational one, so it is necessary to understand the interaction between the legal systems of each Member State, considering all those aspects that, although not explicit, operate concretely in all of them.

To make a bold comparison, here we are faced with something reminiscent of the *lex mercatoria*, i.e. those rules that were consolidated in practice and that, when put in competition with each other, ended up being followed by all "merchants" and on all markets regardless of nationality and even of the "official" recognition of the rules applied.

European (substantive) law operates irrespective of the nationality of the individuals and the places where they act and this is why, especially today, it requires not only synergies and cooperation between Member States but also "alternative" solutions that can actually and concretely operate everywhere, beyond the actual regulatory "recognition" by each system.

This is why the use of the "classical" comparative method is, at least, inadequate. Studying a legal solution adopted in one or more Member States i.e. looking for a "common rule" (as in the case of Principles of European Contract Law ) and thinking of imposing it in a top down process or transplanting it in another legal system without taking into account the systemic differences and the evolution of the specific legal system or, worse, without considering the cultural, social, economic and, above all, political background of each Member State is the best way not to obtain any results, as well as to err in the reconstruction and evaluation of the legal datum. Nowadays legal comparison contemplates not only the single normative data (national, European and international) but also, and above all, studies the connections between the legal rules and normative choices of every 'society', reconstructing also the political-social datum and therefore the effective operation of the rules.

Another weakness of the "traditional" approach to European law (and not only, I would also say to law in general) is the lack of awareness of the substantial diversity in the way law is conceived in the various systems of the Member States (and the world...). Just as, my readers will forgive me, it is not easy to 'export democracy', it must be admitted that one cannot study the European legal system with the spectacles of a "municipal" jurist: one would end up seeing everything emerald-green, as in the Wizard of Oz, but only because one is wearing lenses of that colour.

On the contrary, these differences must be taken into account in the awareness that just because a certain rule or a certain solution works in the United Kingdom, France, Estonia or Italy this does not mean that others must import it or want to import it despite the "supremacy" of European law. Examples of a more or less forced "exportation" of rules can be found everywhere in the world and in recent history. No one or very few look at the concrete fruit of such exportation and especially very few ask the reason for the "rejection" or legal irritation that very often occurs in the receiving countries[14].

The point is that, even though Western legal systems, those of common law and those of civil law that refer to the "Western legal tradition", have in common an idea of law that no one else in the world has, that is, of something that is self-generating and self-justifying, something that is free, indeed completely free from dependence on religious, moral or ethical precepts[15], something in which nothing is created, nothing is destroyed, but everything is transformed by society and without the interference of the legislator except to a limited extent and in particular situations, unfortunately the history and background of the legal systems of each Member State are different, as are to some extent the European population and society. Certainly "globalisation", the freedom of intra-European movement, the development of new information and communication technologies, perhaps even the spread of English as a working language, the circulation of ideas and models, have all undoubtedly contributed to blurring many differences, but, as especially evident today with the emergence of populism, it must be acknowledged that cultural, social and above all systemic differences remain.

Obviously it is difficult to identify all the characteristics of each individual system, but this is precisely the task of the comparatist: to observe the phenomena and trace the origin and evolution of the rules proclaimed and followed, to grasp the weight of the different constituent elements (including and above all the less evident ones) deciphering their significance in relation to the general structure of the individual system, evaluating their actual impact, always taking into account systemic differences but also the small or large events that have contributed to their evolution.

To disregard this apparently indistinguishable mix of small and large events, small and large individual stories that often end up determining the common feeling of each society would be to forget Maitland's lesson and ignore the chaos theory. It is thus up to the comparatist to assess whether and why the flap of a butterfly's wings in London created a hurricane in Brussels[16].

# 2. THE INFLUENCE OF COMMON LAW JUDGES ON THE WORK OF THE EUROPEAN COURT OF JUSTICE AND ON COMMUNITY LAW

As far as this work is concerned, I find it significant that the evolution and growth of the Community (up to 9 members and then increasingly more up to the current 28 minus 1) are linked to a decrease in the actual decision-making ability of the Council and by extension of the Commission itself, with no action being taken by the Parliament.

All of this in the face of an exponential increase in the political-juridical work of the European Court of Justice which in the mid-1970s started a sort of metamorphosis from "judge of the treaties" to a downright judge "on the matter", creatively finding its way into the breakdowns left open by other lazy European institutions. And this is how the European Court of Justice ended up, in my opinion of course, and in terms of the tasks performed, resembling more a House of Lords than a French or German Constitutional Court. I am well aware this statement will lure criticism from many jurists, however just by looking at which and how many cases used to be dealt with before the "divide" caused by the entry of Ireland and the United Kingdom, and which and how many cases after this divide and before the entry of the newcomers, it is clear, based on data, that the Court has really evolved by falling within the influence of common law and by taking advantage of the political-juridical gaps left by the incapacity of the Council to decide or its willingness not to do so[17].

I am not a constitutionalist or a public law expert, and this will be obvious to my twenty-five readers, who may smirk while reading the book. However, if we observe the evolution of the European Union, we cannot fail to note that the six founding Member States were, and still are, Civil law countries of strict "French-German" "faith"[18]. Within the founding Treaty of the European Economic Community, the role of the "Community Courts" was indeed crafted after the legitimation control of the community rules as based on the experience of the administrative[19] and/or constitutional Courts of the Member States.

If I am not mistaken, in the case of European Coal and Steel Community (ECSC) or Euratom, I do not believe that the respective Courts had any interventional powers like those that the European Court of Justice "unleashed" during its initial decades of activity. The outcome of this was a tremendous amount of "leading cases" and even "binding precedents".

You may think this is a bland observation; however, if you look at the size of "European Union law" textbooks, i.e., textbooks about the Institutions of the European Union, which are roughly compared with textbooks about "Substantive European law", i.e., those concerning the "private law" side, you see that the number of pages is twice or even three times that of the former. To elaborate, in the former we find hundreds of cases, against a significantly lower number of controversies in the latter.[20] Although this does not necessarily mean anything from a scientific point of view, I believe that a deeper quantitative and qualitative analysis of the work of the European Court of Justice may prove to be enlightening. Ultimately, it may confirm (or debunk) what is still just my personal view and, perhaps, even a "gut feeling" of mine[21].

The phenomenon has occurred repeatedly throughout law history and it surely also occurred in England where, for example, the ecclesiastical Court found itself a strong and concretely important role by "filling" in the blank spaces either voluntarily or unconsciously opened by the *Curia Regis*. For example, this happened in property and succession matters, wherein: "According to the historical-evolutionary data, it is more appropriate to conclude that common law was not interested in real property, rather than asserting that the ecclesiastical Courts had some sort of exclusive interest. Indeed, ECCLESIASTICAL COURTS HAD BEEN ESTABLISHED to deal with those civil and criminal matters concerning the Church… by applying Church law, and GIVING BIRTH TO A JURISDICTION NOT ALTERNATIVE BUT SPECIAL, SINCE IT TOO WAS DEPENDENT ON THE CROWN AND, CONSEQUENTLY, DESTINED TO FILL THE GAPS LEFT BY COMMON LAW, as it similarly happened shortly after for the other and more peculiar special Courts (such as the commercial Court)… It was then the indifference on the chronicles of movable property of common law and the Crown that gave leeway to ecclesiastical jurisdiction. This indifference can still be seen in doctrine where significant works on personal property and its foundations are lacking compared to more remarkable works on real property and land law"[22].

While I do not want to trespass into a "field" that is not mine[23], I often see and read political scientists and political institutions scholars assessing Court decisions of the highest judicial bodies by rightfully taking into consideration the political aspect of the decision. Moreover, they even succeed in establishing the politically relevant "way of thinking" that a certain Court ends up, more or less voluntarily, complying with[24].

For sure, it is difficult *apertis verbis* to find in the statements of the European Courts a consciousness of them being "lawmaker judges". Usually, they even take pains to specify that their *dictum* is strictly linked to the preservation and application of the norms and the Treaties, and they would never dare adopt the "political" role of legislator-judge. It is difficult to say whether this is a classic case of *excusatio non petita.* Nevertheless, it is certainly doable to say that, on the one hand, this approach derives from the "Napoleonic" way (and the consequent narrow interpretation of the concept of separation of powers) to keep separate "judges" and the political system (which is typical of civil law) and, on the other, it represents the "formal" respect and observance of the judicial role, which in turn is a common law prerogative[25].

Interestingly, from the latter perspective, they specify that, even if "the Common Market is NOT intended to function as the majority of judges consider desirable and expedient, but as prescribed by the Treaties, in the most efficient way however, and by using all possibilities that have a basis in law"[26], this does not rule out the circumstance that "at the same time, there is nothing new or unusual in a Court seeking a solution of a problem which will make things work rather than bring them to a halt". In English law the maxim *"ut res magis valeat quam pereat* goes back at least as far as *Coke on Littleton'*[27]. Hence in the specific case of the European Court of Justice, it may seem like "much misunderstanding stems from a failure to make the essential distinction between the Treaties themselves on the one hand and, on the other, the law which must be observed in their interpretation and observance. (…) [T]he Treaties are the result of political choice, a choice which even now is controversial, just as domestic legislation is frequently the result of controversial political choice. In one sense it may be said that by giving a meaning to a politically motivated text which renders it effective the law is furthering a political end, but this confuses the implementation of a choice with the choice itself and misunderstands the nature of the judicial task. As the Procureur général of the Belgian Cour de Cassation, M. Dumon, has aptly said "a political decision should not be confused with a decision that entails political consequences"[28].

In any case, the Court of Justice, together with the Community, heavily suffered from the arrival of the "common lawyers patrol". Suffice it to say that the excessively complex mechanism of the working and official languages did not stop the English language, once introduced, from "taking over" and becoming the new "*lingua franca*", sometimes generating paradoxical and even hilarious results[29]. Furthermore, mention could be made of the very clever "operation: charm" successfully carried out by common lawyers to win the trust of their "continental" colleagues. It is interesting to remember that the "British patrol" was composed of jurists chosen among those who had a more or less strong "relationship" with the Countries on the Continent and their law. Thus, for example, Adv. General Jean-Pierre Warner, as easily understandable from his own name, was the son of a Frenchman and was educated in France where he lived until he was 14 years old, and, once the war ended, went back to England, Cambridge, where he studied History and then Law. Sir Jean-Pierre Warner became a Barrister (of the prestigious Lincoln's Inn) and after a career in State Administration, as he knew French and French people, he was specifically chosen to represent the United Kingdom at the Court of Justice where he became the first British Advocate-General. Likewise, Lord MacKenzie Stuart married Anne Miller, a university friend he met at the Centre of European Governmental Studies, University of Edinburgh, who was also a jurist and above all very politically active in the Scottish European Movement. Miss Miller knew about community law and surely represented a source of inspiration and advice for her husband, who was appointed judge of the Court of Justice due to his specific university education (the study of law in Scotland is characterized by heavy "Roman" influences, as you may know) and his good knowledge of community law. To continue with a little more gossip, apparently the couple was very notorious in Luxembourg to the point they would "welcome" legendary banquets and carry on a constant political action in favour of a common "European" vision; banquets during which the "judges" would exchange opinions and mix good wine, common sense and common law are used traditionally in English common law to the point that they permitted this system to develop through the traveling judges and the spontaneous "welcome" of local uses and most reasonable decisions. This is a way, not always comprehensible for us, to pleasantly and in non-conflictual terms reason (even between Barristers and Judges) over issues that can get very complex[30].

The work of the "British patrol" was basically oriented towards smoothening and overcoming the self-evident divergences between the Civil law systems and Common law systems and towards mitigating the mistrust of citizens vis-à-vis the common lawyers. Evidently, they had to do so since Lord MacKenzie Stuart, thanks to the efforts of his friend Warner and his wife, was so appreciated for his contribution that he was appointed President of the Court of Justice during the years when its impact had grown tremendously. Moreover, Lord Stuart was among the supporters to the establishment of the "first instance Tribunal" which was launched a few months after the end of his presidency.

Finally, reference can be made, albeit shallowly, to the statistics, particularly how, from 1952 to 1972, the Court of Justice had initially dealt with an average of 50 cases per year, whereas from 1973 onwards there was a twofold escalation at the beginning and an outright explosion from 1979, the year when the Court was requested to lay judgement on 1324 cases. On average, later, the number settled at around 500 cases per year (until 2017)[31].

It may be a coincidence but these numbers could be evidence of an ongoing quantitative increase of the Court claims, immediately after the arrival of the "common lawyers", a growth which cannot even be attributed to an increase of the proceedings "against" (or due to) newcomer States. Apropos, by glancing at the infringement proceedings against Member States, still between 1952 and 2017, the United Kingdom suffered 142 appeals compared to 291 appeals against Germany, 386 against the unsuspicious Belgium, 418 against France and 645 against the "pro-European" Italy.

Above all, during the richest decade in terms of developments and under the MacKenzie Stuart presidency, the Court of Justice had to work with a peculiar composition since the enlargement of the Community to 12 members did not match the "immediate" arrival of judges from the newcomer countries: the role of the "cultural mediator" performed by the *common lawyers* and in particular by the President was reinforced. Moreover, we must consider that the composition of the judging Court during those years (around 21 judges) was a tasty cocktail made up, like a perfect Negroni, of 1/3 of professors, 1/3 of "full judges" from different national Courts and with various experiences, and 1/3 of politicians, economists and administrators who were not necessarily "jurists", actually I would say they were "all but jurists".

As I was saying, this is not the place to analyse the "history" of the composition of the Court but this element surely influenced the evolution (in my opinion, devolution) of the Court's decisions: if judgments are today more "technical" and increasingly more justified upon strict interpretative schemes and juridical-logical reasoning and less upon "reasonableness", this might be due to the increased weight of the full and pure "jurists" with respect to the other components.

I am fully aware that this is an "anecdotal impression" that, as virologists say, is not scientifically proven, yet the current composition of the Court (let alone that of the first-instance Tribunal) comprises 38 judges and advocate generals of whom almost everyone, with the exception of the few representatives of the *common Law* area – who are sadly leaving –, is a graduate and multi-graduate in law, "full" national judges and, mostly, professors of international or European or administrative law[32] while today the Court is composed of 2/3 of (law) professors and 1/3 of judges: we started with a Negroni and we are now drinking a Bellini[33], and the taste is totally different.

# 3. THE RELATIONSHIP BETWEEN COMMUNITY LAW AND DOMESTIC LAW, THE "DISAPPLICATION" ISSUES AND THE *SIMMENTHAL* CASE

By some historical coincidence, Lord MacKenzie Stuart shared his thoughts on the relationship between community law and domestic law, and on the pragmatic role of the Court of Justice through the "Hamlyn Lectures" and through the aforementioned book, *The European Communities and the Rule of Law*, published in April 1977, three months prior to the request for a preliminary ruling and less than one year before the decision on the *Simmenthal* case.

In the Hamlyn Lectures of 1977, Lord MacKenzie addresses the English public and takes stock of the "evolution" and the State of the relationship between community law and domestic law, considering the conceptual differences between *common Law* and *civil Law systems*, in an attempt to explain the job of *"rebuilding"* community rules, the Treaties, and the Court's role.

Starting by stating that "community law has a habit of emerging in unlikely corners. Who at first sight would have thought that an advertisement in a Belgian newspaper for players who might be interested in joining an Italian football club or the issue by French Railways of a card entitling large families to reduced fares could give rise to problems of community law?" and then moving on to highlighting that "among the unspectacular achievements of

Community Institutions I would include those of the Court of Justice of the European communities which, in its decisions, has constantly underscored the basis of legal order on which the communities rest"[34].

And here we are addressing the first point of interest, namely the idea, already overtly recalled in the *Van Gend en Loos v. Nederlands administratie der belastingen* case, that the Community establishes "A NEW LEGAL ORDER FOR THE BENEFIT OF WHICH THE STATES HAVE LIMITED THEIR SOVEREIGN RIGHTS"[35].

Indeed, MacKenzie Stuart clarifies that the "LEGAL ORDER" can translate into a "legal system", but perhaps it would be more coherent to refer to the concept of "*rule of law*". As we all know (or rather, as all comparatists know), the concept of "RULE OF LAW" in English people's mindset is not totally equivalent to its Italian counterpart, "*Stato di diritto*" the French *"Etat de droit"* or German *"Rechtsstaat"*. In fact, as has been sharply observed:

> (...) the rule of law consists in the medieval heritage of the supremacy of rules (*I would personally say of "the Law" i.e. "Diritto, Droit, Derecho instead" – A.N.*), those kinds of rules that the government cannot breach and the Parliament cannot radically change, because in the medieval concept no one "makes" the Law (*even though as per definition "the king cannot do wrong", hence the King himself holds the right to "act" and make his* OWN *law effective, as "his" Government and "his" Court cannot conflict with each other, both of them being "his" outlets*[36]); the Law does not generate from the act of will of a single or a majority as far as (…) (the norm, the rule) it is simply declared or reminded; and only in the case of a missing spot – in a merely supplementary role – the king intervenes via Equity or the Parliament via a Statute. This ancient and timeless law, the common law, is based on consent,

not on that of an assembly, but on the tacit consent of the populace, proved by the usage of the generations[37],

and, if I may add, embodied in the figure of the sovereign who acts as a warden to the "peace of the reign" and "justice".

Based on the above, according to a recent analysis, it would become quite easy to understand the ontological differences between "Rule of law" and "*Stato di Diritto*", the fundamental demarcation line lying on the relationship between the citizen and the State with respect to freedom: "When the former assumes a horizontal type of relationship, where the State ensures the abidance with freedoms and personal rights that exist even prior to the States since they emerged from the bottom, from a society that yearns for freedom, the latter on the contrary emerged from the establishment or transformation of the contemporary State from absolutist to liberal, hence inevitably the State determines the areas wherein freedom and rights can be wielded"[38]. As I often say to students on my comparative legal system course, and by somehow simplifying the concepts to the maximum extent, the difference lies in the fact that *chez nous* in Civil law countries, everything that is not overtly foreseen, permitted or acknowledged by the legislator is, by definition, prohibited or inexistent, whereas for common law the opposite is true, therefore anything that is not explicitly prohibited is always permitted and granted; or at least this is what some of our State officials think[39].

What I want to highlight about MacKenzie Stuart's argument is the idea that THIS "NEW LEGAL SYSTEM" IS BY NO MEANS "NEW": the phrase MacKenzie tells us sounds threatening, because it would suggest that traditional values are eradicated and a new system takes their place, and is consequently "inspired by unknown motives directing our lives along an uncharted path"[40]. We can see here the self-evident cultural legacy of someone who pertains to a society and a legal system that does not tolerate a "revolution", which holds its "spirit"[41] both in the continuum and in the "reasonable" flexibility of adapting to the change of times. This cultural legacy conflicts with, and this clearly explains the statements in the *Van Gend en Loos judgement*, whoever is a "son" of the Revolution and Napoleon (lightly sprinkled with Rousseau), more than the encyclopaedic Enlightenment and the erudite writings and libertarian thought of François-Marie Arouet (known as Voltaire). The Battle of Trafalgar is still going on[42].

On the contrary, what was stated in the *Van Gend en Loos* judgement is to be understood as meaning that "the European Communities do rest upon a system which has its own characteristic – a system which is founded on the principles that those who administer the Communities are themselves subject to limitations imposed by law and that those who are administered have rights in law which must be protected. (…) [They form] a legal order which seeks to assure to the individual certain rights which may be neglected by his national system and which protects him against the arbitrary use of Community power"[43]: accordingly, the "system" is totally coherent and compatible with, yet still different from, the "national" ones pertaining to the Member States.

Indeed, it is also emphasized that "The Community is not a 'State,' at least in any traditional sense of the word. Although the Treaties give it legal personality, it lacks the principal characteristic of a State, which is the ability to act in all matters not specifically excluded (*here the good old conferral, subsidiarity and proportionality principles come into play*[44]). The Community legislative machinery and administration are confined to tasks specifically attributed to them"[45].

This does not mean the Community is born of a simple agreement between States, since it is obvious that the founding Treaty has created something that, as stated in the previous paragraph, had never been seen before, to the point that it led the cautious prof. Nicolaysen to State that the system stemming from the Treaty "is an autonomous legal system, which is intended to give the Community the capacity to act internally and externally, which provides it with fundamental attributes of rule of law and which represents, through its general applicability and through the regular involvement of national Courts, an essential element of integration"[46] without the Community being considered "neither a superstate, nor a quasi-State nor (and this is important) a federal State"[47]; and most importantly as long as the aforementioned ability to integrate following the legal and political autonomy of the Community is intended as the consequence of the TRANSFER of some of the powers heretofore held by Member States[48].

This inevitably leads to the hardly debatable conclusion that "the presumption of jurisdiction lies in favour of the Member States which still preserve their main sovereign powers and remain the principal political entities"[49].

This is the second point worthy of analysis in MacKenzie Stuart's reasoning, namely the idea according to which the Community is a "political" entity, and that the "policies" determined by Member States depend on the law, meaning that both the choices and the development of the

Community are political. Hence, the legal rules derive from this, like a sort of executive instrument.

However, if the choices are of a political nature, likewise the choice to become part of the Community is also a political option, therefore, even though neither Law, nor Courts are entitled to impose political choices on sovereign States. Nevertheless, the political decision to become a member of the community, "prevents" the law of the Member States from being detached from the political choices of the Community, otherwise any choice on the contrary would mean abandoning the Community. This is, more or less, how Lord Denning reasoned when he warned the English Parliament by stating that the *House of Lords* should have always interpreted Statutes as if they were abiding by community law, since an eventual stark contrast with the "political choice" as found in the European Act would have meant an allegation against that choice, hence leaving the Community itself.[50]

Clearly this did not mean that the Parliament or the State were no longer free to legislate or decide, yet it somehow implied an "exacerbation" of the responsibility of changing the political choice of partaking to the Community, notwithstanding the full and utter sovereignty: and if that happened in the Seventies, nowadays it is easier to understand what was, and still is, the tormented Brexit process.

With this in mind, according to the "British" perspective, it is clear that, there is no such thing as a space for a "strong" and "hierarchical" idea of the supremacy of Community law over that of the Member States. Indeed, MacKenzie Stuart himself (as already said, chosen for his obvious pro-Community stances) stated that:

> (...) for my part I dislike the word "supremacy". There is a suggestion in that word of the commander giving orders, of the Austinian superior or someone who speaks *de haut en bas*, a suggestion of a Court sitting on its own particular cloud equidistant from all the Member States and some 5,000 metres above them, issuing edicts which override national traditions and ignore national susceptibilities. Nothing could be further from the truth. The reason why it is essential to adopt the Community solution is not because of any real or pretended existence of a supra-national hierarchy. It arises not from any intrinsic merit of the Community rule in question, but from the very nature and aims of the Community[51]

which, it should be remembered, derives from a political choice. If States have politically chosen to "be together" (*it takes two to tango*, of course), they are not obliged to merely abide by the commitment deriving from the founding treaty – and here neither the monist nor dualist view of the internationalists matters –, but something more and different since the "strength" and the quintessence of the Community (then Union) is born of the political choice of the States which entails the TRANSFER of certain *ad hoc* powers.

In other words, we cannot say the Community/Union is "hierarchically superior" to Member States. We cannot even say there has been a "fusion" of the different systems to shape a unique entity, or two separate but hierarchically tied entities (in the latter case, the relation that ties the different systems to one another in the relationships that fall outside of the obligations with the founding Treaties would not be understandable).

By contrast, the more feasible scenario is based on the observation that the Community/Union represents something that moves in parallel and intersects the systems of the Members States. Like each Member State, also the Community can create rights that must be recognized to all citizens, because Member States have given, politically speaking, a mandate to do so. Stating that "It is only realistic to recognise that the Community legal order, to be effective, must also accommodate legitimate national requirements"[52] is equivalent to saying that the Community/Union is an entity of the same strength as the Member States and their relationship is subject to the quantum entanglement rule or Paul Dirac's equation[53] $(i\partial - m)\psi = 0$.

I will return to this point later on.

What I would like to highlight is that the "common law patrol", and Lord MacKenzie for one, does not use the mental categories of citizens, nor does it refer, even knowing them, to the invoked international law theses[54]. If anything, as I will soon say, it has reinterpreted the evolutionary history of the Community considering its own way of reasoning and according to the typical "logic" of common law, which gives broad experience to the Court in its role of "systematizing" both principles and solutions, also in light of the suggestions coming from sources other than the national legislative one.

To put it in the words of my Mentor Giovanni Criscuoli, the English legal system is open and flexible by nature, albeit provided with a "rubbery" nucleus. Hence, from his point of view, Lord MacKenzie Stuart's statement is perfectly coherent and justifiable: "In the United Kingdom statute law has, doubtlessly, now become more important in many fields than the common law but even when statute innovates it does so against a common law background and reflects evolved social need.

The Community, however, to quote Mr. Shonfield again, is a "political construction which emerges out of a deliberate act of will". Accordingly, "the Community legal order is of a different kind. It would be untrue to say that it has no forensic history, but it is a history with a difference. Essentially, it is a system which starts from a written base and it is on this base that it continues to build. The judicial techniques used in that act of construction may be familiar but they must adapt to new materials and to a new foundation"[55] for example by taking advantage of the unwritten Community law, that is those rules and principles deriving from and common amongst all Member States, albeit not explicitly stated in the Treaties that shape the background and the watermark upon which all Community rules must necessarily be reconstructed: the good faith principle in its objective sense and the "reasonableness", the public order, the "morality of the day", the general terms, the good governance, the human rights, and so on and so forth.

The *loop* is hence clear now. The single national systems react with the Treaties and form a new entity which, in turn, receives from and gives to each national system, creating new entities and developing new energies destined to meeting again, in a chain reaction where the components modify each other, and so on to infinity, indeed as in nuclear fission.

This idea is obviously quite different from the idea popular among internationalists – I would dare say the "Continental" ones – according to whom Community law is created by fusing several nuclei originating from Member States "through a limitation of their own powers" and the obligation to respect the treaties; and it does not matter, as previously stated, if we want to follow a "monist" or "dualist" view since the result would be the same: in any case Community law is superior to domestic law even if this position does not sit well with the never-doubted independence and sovereignty of the Member States themselves[56].

The matter is more complicated than can be portrayed here. However, it is clear to me that among British jurists it is totally normal to presume the co-existence of and fission between several nuclei or systems of rules and principles, which self-fuel and reproduce, even overlapping without prevaricating, while they integrate because this is how the machinery of common law works.

Besides, as we can infer from what MacKenzie Stuart has written, the British vision of the relationship between national law and Community law suffers from the mental categories and the pragmatic and only slightly theoretical way of dealing with problems, which is typical of that system; if we add the widely different education of the British jurists with respect to the traditional and scholastic education of continental jurists we can easily comprehend how the idea of the supremacy of Community law based on "monist" and "dualist" theories found by the internationalists and based on a presumed "limitation of the power of the State" sounds off-key if not screeching.

Indeed, if we look at the complexity of the English sources of law system, and particularly at the relationship between Statute law and Common law on the one hand and between Common law and Equity on the other, we can easily understand whether and how the "British thought" has influenced the decisions of the European Court of Justice; furthermore we can understand whether, from our point of view, this would allow us to envisage a different relationship from the one traditionally assumed (and taken for granted) between the power of States and Community law, perhaps even by resorting, as seems possible to me with due proportion, to categories in use in private law[57].

I cannot, nor do I want to, describe in any depth the relationships between Statute law, Common law and Equity also because it is a well-known subject. I will therefore only recall some fundamental passages and writings[58] on the issue, which provide us with the context wherein the British approach to Community law, or better the work of judges such as MacKenzie Stuart, matured.

As shown for the English and the common lawyers the coexistence of different systems and sources which act on an equal basis is not something traumatic or at least it is not resolved according to supremacy or abdication and limitation of the powers which in theory cannot even be put into discussion: the conflicts, when they arise, are resolved "by taking English leave" – though the English actually say: by taking French leave – bypassing the problems or using technical ploys which obtain the desired concrete result and even only apparently save the intrinsic logic of the system.

In *Comparazione giuridica e Diritto europeo*, Luigi Moccia clarifies the meaning behind the "Law – Equity" dualism which translates into that "long-lasting separation of two systems of rules, principles and protection mechanisms, which is still relevant to the structure of law in England... in turn characterized by two regimes and legal categories, with the due classifications and qualifications, of a terminological and conceptual nature"[59]. This coexistence, which is not always peaceful, is difficult to grasp for a *post-napoleonic* jurist if it is true that "if someone were compelled to explain the essence of civil law to a common lawyer in one sentence, he could perhaps say that civil law is what common law would have been if it had never known a Court of chancery. It is true that the answer would hardly be helpful, the picture suggested being probably beyond the imagination of a common lawyer. The picture of conflicting and coexisting jurisdictions is equally inconceivable to a Latin or even a German lawyer, who believes in the *Einheit der Rechtsordnung*, the uncompromising and sometimes cruel unity of the legal order"[60].

Coming to the relationship itself and trying to overcome the "unconceivable", it is sufficient to recall that, if common law is the product of the work of the judges, it is in theory the manifestation of Royal power speaking through its judges. However, at the same time, also the Court of Chancery is a manifestation of sovereignty: using an expression by the iconic Count of Nottingham, the sovereign is a source of justice and grace, of law and equity and these have been waived to the Courts as God is the source of light and waives it to the Sun and the Moon[61].

These two systems, despite the Judicature Acts 1873-1875, albeit formally reunited, are still separate and work on principles sometimes different but always in the name of the Sovereign. To the extent that: "Equity follows the law", that it must abide by the common law even when it works towards it, correcting its solutions or filling its gaps. It will therefore never disown it, just as it will not disown or cancel the subjective rights existing under it. But it will paralyse it, blocking the exercise of the corresponding subjective rights, by appropriate technical instruments as in injunction or set aside. This latter instrument, as widely known, for example, serves the purpose of "putting away" a contract which, even if valid under Common law, is declared ineffective under Equity. The result is the same as declaring the contract null and void, since in practice saying that a contract is null and void and therefore cannot produce effects or saying that a contract is valid but cannot produce effects is actually the same thing. The point is that the Court of Equity cannot formally go against the Common law Court, but must find an alternative route by "disapplying" the Common law rules and "applying" the principle of Equity. Equity principles seem "special" compared to the "general" principles of Common law, hence they are applied "on preference" where a new circumstance posed under the judgement of the Court, perfectly fits the scope of the judged precedent: if it were not so, Common law would be full effective and should be applied without delay. In other terms, Common law rule is valid and applicable to all future circumstances unless exactly the same circumstance is already recognized under Equity. Both systems remain diversified and operate by regulating possible overlapping under said mechanism.

Moreover, we are talking about systems that do not interact with the "fusion" of two separate entities, but with a "fission" giving birth to ever new interactions, the development of new rules and the application of new principles. An example of this is easily seen in the regulation of trusts. The latter, originally used for special needs, has become a complex instrument covering various situations and has ended up changing the typologies of succession, family, patrimonial and commercial law.

By another historical coincidence Lord MacKenzie Stuart was the son of prof. MacKenzie Stuart, the author of a successful and important volume on Trust[62] and also a very notorious lecturer at the University of Aberdeen.

With no intention to give too much weight to historical "incidents" and the impact of a single man on events, it is obvious here that those common lawyers who arrived in Luxembourg (and English jurists as a whole) were aware of the fact that: *i)* Member States held full sovereignty; *ii)* the relationship between the Community and the Member State was basically of a political nature; *iii)* the so-called "new legal order" was based more on the concept of rule of law rather than that of *stato di diritto, état de droit* or *rechtsstaat* ; *iv)* there was no fusion between the national system and the Community one; *v)* there was no supremacy (hierarchy, based on both monist and dualist theories of international law, etc.) of Community law over the law of the Member States; *vi)* there was no limitation of State powers but rather a, political and voluntary, "transfer" within the scope of the subsidiarity principle; *vii)* the Community legal system was peer-to-peer to the legal system of the Member State since both of these are valid as sources of law; *viii)* the two systems could perfectly integrate and cohabit as in the secularly relationship between Statute law and Common law and more importantly between Equity and Common law, and any overlapping problems could be resolved in accordance with the rules of the Treaties, the subsidiarity principle and the technical mechanism used to resolve similar conflicts in Equity and Common law.

Taking this background into consideration, as I was saying, some months following the publication of the "Hamlyn Lectures", Lord MacKenzie Stuart took part in the drafting of the Simmenthal case judgement, which was specifically about the principle of the direct effect of Community norms – an issue already dealt with in the Van Gen den Loos case.

We all know that this decision established the principle according to which the national judge, when dealing with a conflict between statutory norms (even *ex post*) and Community norms (in particular the directly effective ones), is obliged to disapply domestic law and apply community law.

As mentioned previously, the Court, chaired by the expert H. KUTSCHER (a graduate in Political Sciences and law, he had an administrative role in the German government where he had gained a lot of experience and subsequently served as a judge in the Bundesverfassungsgericht), was composed of two judges and jurists of the common law area, and LECTURERS the likes of PIERRE PESCATORE (a Luxembourg man, former director and Permanent Secretary of the Ministry of Foreign Affairs of Luxembourg, Special Professor and professor of European Community law), GIACINTO BOSCO (Italian, the oldest member, Professor of international law and (above all) senator, and more than once a Minister in various ministries), MAX SORENSEN (Danish Professor of International law and Constitutional law, with great experience in politics expanded further in London at the Permanent Court of Arbitration) and ANDREAS DONNER (Dutch Professor of Constitutional and Administrative law, son of the Dutch Prime Minister, President of the Court who decided the *Van Gen den Loos* case). The advocate general was GERHARD REISCHL (German national Judge with great experience, Secretary of State and member of the Bundenstag).

The judgement apparently fits within the reasoning of those precedents judged by the same Court of Justice.

In paragraph 17, the judgement reads "*le disposizioni e atti [del Trattato e delle istituzioni] fanno parte integrante, con rango supe-*

*riore rispetto alle norme interne, dell'ordinamento giuridico vigente nel territorio dei singoli Stati membri*" [63] (i.e: "the provisions and acts [of the Treaty and of the institutions] form an integral part of the legal order in force in the territory of the individual Member States, with higher rank than internal rules"). Moreover, *"il riconoscere una qualsiasi efficacia giuridica ad atti legislativi nazionali che invadano la sfera nella quale si esplica il potere legislativo della Comunità, o altrimenti incompatibili con il diritto comunitario, equivarrebbe (...) a negare sotto questo aspetto il carattere reale d'impegni incondizionatamente ed irrevocabilmente assunti, in forza del Trattato, dagli Stati membri mettendo così in pericolo le basi stesse della Comunità"* (i.e. "to recognise any legal effectiveness of national legislative acts which encroach upon the sphere in which the Community's legislative power is exercised, or which are otherwise incompatible with Community law, would be tantamount (...) to denying in this respect the real character of commitments unconditionally and irrevocably entered into by the Member States under the Treaty, thereby undermining the very foundations of the Community").

The formulation used is somewhat hazy since, on the one hand, it admits that Community law norms are of a "higher rank" (*Rango superiore*) and, on the other, that this "superiority" is the consequence of the fact that these norms pertain to those of "exclusive competence" of the Community.

In my opinion, this is exactly the point which sparks interest the most because there is no *apertis verbis* (or even implied) reference to the limitation of the power of the States, and there is no explanation, other than a minor reference to the political duties of the Member States, in what is concretely meant by "disapplication"[64], in view of the fact that if Community norms are higher-ranking that domestic ones, the latter should be null or at least "not constitutionally[65] compatible" with Community norms[66].

My Mentor, already mentioned herein, taught me that it is always better to check the original sources in order both to better understand and try to avoid possible interpretive issues. This is true especially at a European level, since the translation of a decision into different official languages is often contextualized by the "language of the case". However, the decision, in turn, is the outcome of a discussion that probably took place between the judges of the Court in a common language, which is not always fully mastered on the one hand, and on the other hand does not necessarily appropriately translate the legal concepts and contents of the terminology used. This may be even more true in the specific case at stake, where Italian was the language of the controversy to be adjudicated, a Luxemburger was the drafting judge, a German was the Advocate General, with the two remaining judges of the Court being respectively a British man from Scotland (a native English speaker also perfectly fluent in French) and an Irish man. The matter is even more tricky if viewed from an Italian perspective, because the decision has, at least in the "Italian" version, been used for a lot of decisions even by our Court of Cassation and the Constitutional Court and particularly in the "Granital case".

Taking into consideration Lord MacKenzie's "profession of faith" in his Hamlyn Lectures and the abovementioned considerations, I decided to compare the Italian text with the French and English ones, in order to be sure that the meaning of the Italian terms matched that of the French and English terms.

Paragraph 17 sounds pretty similar in both the Italian

> (...) *in forza del principio della preminenza del diritto comunitario, le disposizioni del Trattato e gli atti delle istituzioni, qualora siano direttamente applicabili, hanno l'effetto, nei loro rapporti col diritto interno degli Stati membri, non solo di rendere «ipso jure» inapplicabile, per il fatto stesso della loro entrata in vigore, qualsiasi disposizione contrastante della legislazione nazionale preesistente, ma anche – in quanto dette disposizioni e detti atti fanno parte integrante, con rango superiore rispetto alle norme interne, dell'ordinamento giuridico vigente nel territorio dei singoli Stati membri – di impedire la valida formazione di nuovi atti legislativi nazionali, nella misura in cui questi fossero incompatibili con norme comunitarie*

and French

> (...) *qu'au surplus, en vertu du principe de la primauté du droit communautaire, les dispositions du traité et les actes des institutions directement applicables ont pour effet, dans leurs rapports avec le droit interne des États membres, non seulement de rendre inapplicable de plein droit, du fait même de leur entrée en vigueur, toute disposition contraire de la législation nationale existante, mais encore – étant que ces dispositions et actes font partie intégrante, avec rang de priorité, de l'ordre juridique applicable sur le territoire de chacun des États membres – d'empêcher la formation valable de nouveaux actes législatifs nationaux dans la mesure où ils seraient incompatibles avec des normes communautaires*

versions when we consider the most important statement in Italian *"con rango superiore rispetto alle norme interne"* and in French *"avec rang de priorité"*, although the latter, ironically, does not mention any domestic norms, nor does it use the word "superior", which would have catered for a stronger purpose.

On closer inspection the word *priorité* remarkably recalls[67] the concept of "precedence" or "prevalence" which is more neutral and generic especially when not referring to any domestic norms. Saying that Community norms are "superior" to those of the Member States is consistent with the precedents of that same Court of Justice, and is shallower than strongly declaring the existence of a "strict hierarchy", in addition neither constitutionally nor politically justified. Then, if we look at the English version[68]:

> (...) *furthermore, in accordance with the principle of the* PRECEDENCE *of Community law, the relationship between provisions of the Treaty and directly applicable measures of the institutions on the one hand and the national law of the Member States on the other is such that those provisions and measures not only by their entry into force render automatically* INAPPLICABLE *any conflicting provision of current national law but – in so far as they are an integral part of, and* TAKE PRECEDENCE IN, *the legal order applicable in the territory of each of the Member States – also preclude the valid adoption of new national legislative measures to the extent to which they would be incompatible with Community provisions*

it is clear that that this statement is almost identical to the French version, that is "take precedence in" with no reference to domestic norms. Moreover, the whole paragraph sounds perfectly in line with MacKenzie Stuart's theses on the relationship between Community law and domestic law, which were widely spread amongst British jurists.

The difference between these texts is even clearer when we reach the "pivotal" paragraph (no. 21), which is the core of the decision, that is the statement saying:

> (...) *qualsiasi giudice nazionale, adito nell'ambito della sua competenza, ha l'obbligo di applicare integralmente il diritto comunitario e di tutelare i*

*diritti che questo attribuisce ai singoli,* DISAPPLICANDO LE DISPOSIZIONI EVENTUALMENTE CONTRASTANTI DELLA LEGGE INTERNA, *sia anteriore sia successiva alla norma comunitaria.*

In the French version

(...) *qu'il découle de l'ensemble de ce qui précède que tout juge national, saisi dans le cadre de sa compétence, a l'obligation d'appliquer intégralement le droit communautaire et de protéger les droits que celui-ci confère aux particuliers,* EN LAISSANT INAPPLIQUÉE TOUTE DISPOSITION ÉVENTUELLEMENT CONTRAIRE DE LA LOI NATIONALE, *que celle-ci soit antérieure ou postérieure à la règle communautaire*

the word "disapplicando" is translated by "*EN LAISSANT INAPPLIQUEE*" which, in my opinion, implies an intrinsic "validity" of domestic law which does not cease to be recognized outside of the specific field covered by Community norms.

In the English version

(...) *It follows from the foregoing that every national Court must, in a case within its jurisdiction, apply Community law in its entirety and protect rights which the latter confers on individuals* AND MUST ACCORDINGLY SET ASIDE ANY PROVISION OF NATIONAL LAW *which may conflict with it, whether prior or subsequent to the Community rule*

the full text of paragraph n. 21 is extremely simplified and the word *"disapplicando"* is turned into a softer "*SET ASIDE*". However, this is also typically British, so typically related to Common law, since the tools set aside have been used especially in the case of overlaps and/or conflicts between Equity and Common law rules.

As hard as I tried, I could not find any prior judgement to the Simmenthal case using the terms set aside, among the countless Court of Justice decisions: if this is true, it would confirm that the terms and the underlying concept, were introduced by the "common law patrol" judges and maybe even by Lord MacKenzie Stuart himself. Consequently, the Simmenthal judgement is more deeply entrenched in English legal tradition than in Civil law.

To be honest, the word "disapplication" does not seem to be very common amongst Civil law jurists, or even less so, if we consider its British meaning, hence according to the concept of "set aside".

It probably explains the "resistance" of the Constitutional Court in the Granital case[69] where there is an obsessive repetition of the idea of disapplication of domestic law in favour of Community law if a domestic norm conflicts with a Community norm. The justification is the same as the previous one, i.e. that we are dealing with two different systems not yet coordinated and that our system has consented to a limitation of powers as per art. 11 of the Constitution.

Although this reasoning is (more or less) coherent with the "Italian version" of the Simmenthal case, it would not be so, in my opinion, if we took into consideration the English version. Ultimately, it is true that, based on the English experience, it is not possible to provide a different interpretation, without reconstructing a more linear and coherent relationship between domestic (Italian) law and Community law.[70]

Admittedly, my friend Alan Watson would probably notice that here, concretely and particularly in the Granital case, I think our Courts performed, totally involuntarily, a transplant of concepts, alien to the system, yet justified in validity according to the internal instruments of the receiver and, consequently, not fully coherent with the context of the "donor".

I am once again going back to the issue of the composition of the Courts: certainly, I could never doubt the great science and education of the learned and distinguished judges who were (and are) called to partake in our Constitutional Court. I however notice that in the Granital case the Court was composed of Doctors and *grand-commis* Aldo Corasaniti, Francesco Saja and Arnaldo Maccarone, the notorious politicians Brunetto Bucciarelli Ducci and Oronzo Reale, two judges coming from the Council of State and the Court of Auditors, namely Antonino De Stefano and Guglielmo Roehrseen, and finally the well-known (in Italy, at least) professors Leopoldo Elia, Livio Paladin, Antonio La Pergola, Virgilio Andrioli, Giuseppe Ferrari, Giovanni Conso and Ettore Gallo; the latter being public law, criminal law, criminal procedure law, civil procedure law, parliamentary law and constitutional law professors, respectively.

Despite their questionably extensive and encyclopedic knowledge, none of them could be ascribed within the "comparative law" scientific field except pr. La Pergola – teacher of Public law institutions, LL.M. at Harvard, teacher of comparative government at the John Hopkins University in Bologna, one of the three lecturers together with Bognetti and Tesauro of American Public law and great connoisseur of United States law which is, however, far from having the "purity" of the English system[71]; not bad, of course.

With this, I do not mean, nor could I, that these judges did not know the English, French or German systems; on the contrary, these great Mentors had an encyclopedic knowledge so broad that is difficult to find nowadays. However, we can legitimately presume that comparative techniques and the study of the English system in particular and the foreign systems in general, were not really their "center of interest", as they say.

This is why I talked about an "involuntary" transplant of the disapplication concept. Perhaps there was no rejection, yet surely some sort of "legal irritation" occurred and, at least for me, there are still many doubts.

# 4. THE LEGISLATIVE POWER OF THE STATE: A FORGOTTEN JUDGEMENT OF THE COURT OF CASSATION AND A LITTLE-KNOWN JUDGEMENT OF THE QUEEN'S BENCH DIVISION

The resistance of the Italian Constitutional Court, before its (almost) final surrender, to the "supremacy" of Community law has attracted strong criticism and few favourable opinions. After the Granital ruling, the few critics definitively drowned in the maelstrom of the champions of European Union almightiness.

On the contrary, in the United Kingdom Lord MacKenzie Stuart's ideas, which were welcomed favourably by most of English jurists, were increasingly consolidating in the pragmatic vision of the Courts, which in turn had the chance to clarify their thoughts on the relationship with the Union.

This happened in particular when, after the Maastricht Treaty, a debate on the "Royal prerogatives" started blossoming. The question fundamentally entailed a risk: that these prerogatives were being used as a compromise and, therefore, were being compromised. This, for the United Kingdom, meant the desire to or not to accept the "constitutionalization" of the European Union. However, these fears turned out to be baseless, since, as history tells us, the "European Constitution" – as it was flamboyantly and rather recklessly called – was crippled by The Netherlands and France.

Still thanks to those historical coincidences, which here however start to matter like Agata Christie's "three pieces of evidence", around the years when the principle stated in the Francovich case[72] was spreading, two more or less similar judgements were delivered in Italy and in the United Kingdom, involving the issue of the "prerogative" of the Parliament and the Crown, respectively.

For reasons of lengthiness and personal limitations, I cannot delve into the debate on State prerogatives. I will solely build on these two judgements to link back to the issue about the relationship between domestic law and Community law.

I will start with the almost forgotten judgement no. 4915 of 1/4/2004 delivered by our Italian Supreme Court (Corte di Cassazione), which, depending on the perspectives, was more of a sore thumb or a bad egg, than an April fool, amongst the decisions concerning the relationships with the Community legal system.

The case originated from an apparently insignificant issue: on June 12, 1991, Mr. Massimo Della Minola bought at his personal domicile some books from one of the salespersons of Public Marketing S.r.l; a couple of days after this purchase, Della Minola informed the salesperson he would withdraw from the contract, as per arts. 4 and 5 of Directive 577/85/EEC on contracts negotiated away from business premises. However, Publi Marketing contested the buyer's right to withdraw. Hence Della Minola sued the seller before the Praetor of Pietrasanta (Tuscany) who, on March 3, 1994, refused the claimant's request, his decision being based on the fact that said Directive had not yet been "implemented" by the Italian legal system. Since he lost his case, Della Minola did not appeal the decision, since he merely paid 750,000 Italian lire, as a compromise with Publi Marketing, obtaining also the consensual resolution of the contract.

Having closed the deal with Publi Marketing, Della Minola changed his "victim", by turning his attention to Pietrasanta's Justice of Peace. Therefore, he took the Italian State to Court, in the person of the then Prime Minister (President of the Council of Ministers), stating that he had been damaged (amidst actual transaction costs, procedural costs to the praetor, and not even a bound book on display in the bookshops) for a total amount of 2,000,000 Italian lire as a consequence of the delayed implementation of the directive by the State, which actually took place on 15/1/1992.

Nonetheless (or maybe for this same cause) the motives exposed by the defence of the State called to Court, the Justice of Peace on September 30, 1998, decided in favour of the claimant, holding that, pursuant to art. 2043 of the Italian Civil Code and according to the "superior equity principle", the Italian State had to respond for the damage suffered by Della Minola. Just 11 years from the facts that caused the case under scrutiny, the Italian Supreme Court issued a final decision, where the appeal lodged by the Presidency of the Council was upheld and Della Minola's counter-motives were dismissed. Ironically, Mr Della Minola would have been better off if he had settled for the purchase of the book, which he had later rejected.

As I said, this sentence was passed in silence and was essentially forgotten. However, despite the considerable research conducted, I found only a few critical notes among scholars[73], all of which were focused above all on condemning the apparent disclaimer by the Court of Cassation of the principle of State liability for failure to implement Community directives.

This last issue is of remarkable interest and often approached by Scholars, but, in my view, the principle delivered in the well-known Francovich case (about which I can only suggest reading the enlightening pages written by Ermanno Calzolaio[74]) is not the pivotal point of the sentence that, here and now, is being examined.

It is true that not much can be taken from the few pages of the reasoning and the maxim might even be incoherent, yet in my opinion the highlight of the reasoning followed by the Court is, on the one hand, tied to the facts themselves and the inherent concepts of art. 2043 Italian Civil Code[75] and, on the other, it is tied to the fact that the Court remarked, as was necessary, the sovereignty of the Parliament and the legislator. Ironically, here the "Government" had to defend the sovereignty of the role of the Parliament and the legislator when, even before this judgement, the role of the Parliament was quite secondary and unremarkable. But that is another story.

Returning to the present judgment, I believe that the plaintiff played a significant role. Of course, although I am not saying that those who bring Article 2043 of the Civil Code to trial must have clean hands, as in the case of Equity across the Channel, but *de minimis* that plaintiff must not 'take advantage' of the situation.

Anyway, I think, the conditions for the application of *neminem laedere* are even missing here, since, by assuming that there has been no damage at all, it lacks the element of illogical injustice and unreasonable disproportion between the acts or failure to act of the parties. Ultimately, what I mean is that the behaviour of the claimant does not appear to be linear: he sued the Praetor and the selling company but, after he lost, he did not appeal, rather he accepted a transaction. Consequently, he asked the State to pay for the transaction and the legal and transaction costs that he had decided to face. In short it looks like he wanted to take "two bites of the cherry" and this is, other than for other technical reasons, unreasonable and unjust[76] to the point it rules out the injustice of the claimed damages.

Of course, we do not know whether the plaintiff's behaviour was really a "hidden motive" to tilt the odds of victory against him, and we know that history and judgments cannot be made with "ifs and buts". However, in this case the Court of Cassation excludes the responsibility of the State, not by "debunking" the general principle as in the *Francovich* case, but rather by reaffirming a very obvious principle according to which if the Italian State is sovereign and THE ITALIAN PARLIAMENT HAS THE POWER TO "MAKE" LAW, THEN IT IS ALSO FREE NOT TO MAKE THEM, since there is no hierarchical "subordination" to the European Union.

We might say in this case that the same principle of peoples' and parties' autonomy is still valid: full freedom is not just about being able TO DO something but also about being able NOT to do something. If the Parliament (the Legislator, I would say) is in any way obliged to make law, it would not be free to pursue authority in the name of the people following art. 1 of our Constitution[77].

Regarding the case under scrutiny someone could argue that there is actually a limitation of sovereignty (according to art. 11 of the Constitution) consequently to becoming part of the European Union; someone could say that it is mandatory to adjust to European Directives and the missing adjustment causes liability of the State towards the citizen according to the precedent *Francovich* case. On this last point there are two critical notes to the case under scrutiny. However, as I was saying, I do not believe the Court of Cassation in any way doubted the precedent

*Francovich* case and the obligation following the treaties of adjusting the system to Community directives. Chances are the explicit reference to the precedents recalled in the sentence of the same Court of Cassation derailed the critics; but even in this case the reasoning refers to a general principle, actually very general of our legal system and it does not concern the issue raised in the *Francovich* case.

I believe that the judges of the Court of Cassation have been more than clear: "The Constitution in providing fundamental norms on the organization and on the functioning of the State, regulates the legislative function, splitting it between the government and the parliament, IN ITS BEING AN AFFIRMATION OF POLITICAL POWER, HENCE FREE IN ITS PURPOSES AND NOT COMPELLED TO ANY JUDICIAL REVIEW. Consequently, in executing its political power, NO PERSONAL SITUATION PROTECTED BY AN INDIVIDUAL CAN BE PURSUED, HENCEFORTH IT MUST BE RULED OUT that from Community system norms can stem – to the Italian system – ANY RIGHT OF THE INDIVIDUAL TO EXERCISE LEGISLATIVE POWER and in any case the qualification in terms of wrongdoing, according to art. 2043 of the Civil Code, against the Person-State, of any composition of the System-State".

In brief the Court explicitly States that the Parliament is free and so it remains, and it holds the authority to make (OR NOT TO MAKE) law and there is no right of the individual to obtain a law. The Court also implicitly States that from Community law, it however, emerges that THE ADJUSTMENT OF THE DOMESTIC SYSTEM CAN BE PURSUED WITH ANY INSTRUMENT and it should be absolutely pursued by enacting a law; which in the case in point the claimant could not sue the State for not making any adjustment law, since there were alternative routes.

This is not really a central issue for the purposes of this work, yet it is still useful to precisely understand the target of the Court of Cassation. Basically, and here I go back to Della Minola's behaviour, at the end of the day the claimant could have solved the matter differently, for example by challenging the Praetor's decision, which was in favour of Publi Marketing[78]. Moreover, no one had forced the same claimant to solve the first dispute with a transaction, hence the inconceivability of addressing the transaction as a "failure to act" of the State even just as a simple causal link (something that had been strongly highlighted in the grounds of the appeal by the Presidency of the Council of Ministers and welcomed by the Court of Cassation). I would also add that Della Minola, or rather his lawyer, could have better claimed for compensation for a total lack of tuning by the State[79], thus not linking it to a delay in providing a law implementing said directive.

There are still some points to ponder upon in art. 11 of the Italian Constitution and upon the "due limitation of powers of a system to ensure peace and justice among the Nations". Actually, in this particular case, the Italian Supreme Court just recalled the principle of State sovereignty which, regardless of art. 11, has not apparently been questioned by the Treaties of the Community and the Union. Cautiously, the Court solely stated the inadmissibility of the claim for damages as a consequence of a lack of or delay in providing a law implementing Community law (an aim which, again, could have been pursued with other instruments and, in theory, even by the judge of first instance with a "compliant" interpretation). Having said that, I still suspect that using art. 11 to justify the superiority of Community law over domestic law is "*plus royaliste que le roi*".

I am not totally convinced of the fact that the relationship in question could really generate a limitation of powers, but rather a transfer or even a delegation of powers. At the end of the day, when we look at various national legislations of Member States and refer back to the decisions of the European Court of Justice, I have not seen any reference to hierarchical superiority of Community norms and limitation of powers, or any waiver of independence and sovereignty by any Member State[80]. Except for the "Italian vulgate", of course!

This is exactly the issue raised in the case decided by the English Queen's Bench Division in 1993 that saw the Queen against Rees-Mogg, Secretary of State for Foreign and Commonwealth affairs[81].

This decision was kept maintained for over 15 years and it recently made a comeback due to the so-called Brexit with the well-renowned judgement on the Miller case[82]. Precisely, the judgement where *the former House of Lords, now Supreme Court,* stated that withdrawal from a Treaty like the European one, without asking the Parliament for "authorization", does not fall within Crown and Government ministers' prerogatives. The Supreme Court apparently distinguished this case from that of 1993, however reaffirming the main focus, as the Crown and the Government ministers can exercise their prerogatives, at most delegating them with no prior "consent" from the Parliament and just for limited issues.

The case in question, the one decided by the QBD, which someone has excessively described "as the most important constitutional case for three hundred years", was brought by Lord Rees Mogg, a well-known pro-Brexit Tory member of Parliament, immediately after the signature of the

Maastricht Treaty, specifically arguing that "by ratifying Title V of the Treaty, the Government would be transferring part of Royal Prerogative to Community institutions without statutory authority, namely, the power to conduct foreign and security policy" which would have been impossible and practically excluded if not forbidden by English constitutional rules, since it would have practically meant an "abdication and waiver" of the Crown's own exercise of powers.

It is to be pointed out that this particular case was considered specious since, as it was later brought up by the defence of the Crown, the United Kingdom had not entered into the "Social Policy Protocol", meaning that the problem did not even exist. If anything, it was a byproduct and consequential to the adoption of the whole Treaty and Title V in particular. Indeed, the Crown argued that the Treaty had to be considered as a *unicum*, hence comprising the protocols too, as long as they were "applicable" to the United Kingdom and no "alteration of the domestic system" would occur.

However, in reality, the case was all about the "philosophical" and "constitutional" issue of eventually transferring the Royal prerogatives to Community institutions.

Lord Justice Lloyd immediately States that the issue brought by Rees Mogg is surely interesting albeit feeble. Indeed, after recalling some articles of Title V of the Maastricht Treaty[83] "*to give the flavour*", Justice Lloyd goes immediately to the question brought by the claimant: "By English common law, the Crown, he says, is incapable of abandoning, or transferring, any of its ancient prerogative powers, without statutory enactment". In fact, Rees Mogg makes the case with a significant quantity of persuasive authorities and precedents to which the Crown defence skilfully responded. Justice Lloyd recalls the precedent case *Blackburn v The Attorney General,*[84] wherein Blackburn claimed that, by signing the Treaty of Rome, the British Government had perpetually transferred part of Royal and Parliament prerogative powers and this fact was openly violating the law. In that case, Lord Denning, with a curious statement resembling that of our Court of Cassation in the Della Minola case, pointed out as follows: "Mr. Blackburn acknowledged the general principle, but he urged that this proposed treaty is in a category by itself, in that it diminishes the sovereignty of Parliament over the people of this country. I cannot accept the distinction. The general principle applies to this treaty as to any other. The treaty-making power of this country rests not in the Courts, but in the Crown; that is, Her Majesty acting upon the advice of her Ministers. When Her Ministers negotiate and sign a treaty, even a treaty of such paramount importance as this proposed one, they act on behalf of the country as a whole. THEY EXERCISE THE PREROGATIVE OF CROWN. Their action in so doing cannot be challenged or questioned in these Courts".

According to the foregoing, which has been confirmed by other subsequent decisions, Justice Lloyd concludes by arguing that Title V of the Maastricht Treaty "cannot be regarded as a transfer of prerogative powers. (…) TITLE V DOES NOT ENTAIL AN ABANDONMENT OR TRANSFER OF PREROGATIVE POWERS; BUT AN EXERCISE OF THOSE POWERS".

There are countless issues that could be discussed on "Crown prerogative" and on the sovereignty of the State and the powers of the Parliament, however it would be too broad and out of place for the purposes of this work.

The point of interest is that the judgement of the English Court decided upon the exclusion of a transfer or limitation of powers[85], following the signature of Community and European Union Treaties, on the contrary arguing that by signing those treaties power is exercised in that it falls within Crown (or State) prerogative to delegate – it is no coincidence that the term used is exactly "delegation" – to other institutions the power to manage and initiate on certain issues, clearly within a definite scope and always limited and subsidiary in nature.

This statement perfectly falls within the concept outlined by Lord MacKenzie Stuart twenty years earlier, and it makes us better understand how common law jurists see the relationship between Community law and domestic law: a perspective which does not take into consideration neither the possibility of a fusion or blending between systems, nor that "multilevel" coexistence. On the contrary, the perspective takes the matter in hand, in light of the historical experience of ancient common law. That is, they point at a non-conflictual yet collaborative relationship between the Member State and the Union when the latter, which represents a source of law, entering in contact with national law, generates and nurtures never-ending new legally relevant situations, always calling for different reactions and protections.

# 5. THE FISSION OF COMMUNITY LAW

It is time to conclude this long journey that I have been trying to make riding the "diminutive donkey" used by Hercule Poirot to avoid the consequences of the sudden and tortuous turns that have entailed untangling the many different visions of the "common European path" compound.

Precisely in this last regard, I would like to say that the impression one gets from reading our "Authorities" (Authors and legal Scholars) is that of a clammy and even self-referential closure on theoretical constructions of an "area" and categories in use among jurists (more or less hard and pure): there is an attempt, therefore, to justify the dynamics resulting from the formation of the Union and its precursors on the basis of a vision of the State and State law, which could only be appropriate if the European Union were one of the many International Organizations or if the Member States were still the "modern" ones (i.e. Nations with National Powers and a National legal system) born out of the French Revolution and sons of codifications and Constitutions.

I also get the feeling that this approach is a by-product of the Italian "education of the jurist", hence lacking important political aspects that are actually at the core of the European Union. Of course, I am not doubting, nor would I for personal limits, the work of the Constitutional Court or the "pro-Europe" jurists at large. However, I am afraid that, once we look through the jurist's lenses, everything appears to be green as in *The Wizard of Oz* and the relationship between the European Union and the Member States cannot even be seen in its colourful and varied political nature.

My point is that, if we still address the European question with the jurist's small toolbox and we leave out the historian's and political scientist's, we risk adopting an excessively enclosed perspective; therefore, it is natural albeit not conclusive to look for justifications and assume theories that may be meaningful in juridical terms but stop being coherent in the face of the actual political fact.

Starting from the limitations or transfer of sovereignty which, as the previous pages have shown, is not so widespread in the "brother" States and might even be deemed a legal-linguistic misunderstanding. As I was saying, the other States do not question the sovereignty of the single State, however they accept, with all due considerations, the priority of Community law, in Italy we use art. 11 of the Constitution to "constitutionalize" Community norms and ascribe them under the "limitation of sovereignty" umbrella.

I am not a constitutionalist, nor a public law jurist, however I do not think it takes much to admit that, regardless of the reciprocity principle that is not at all abided by here, art. 11 of the Italian Constitution was formulated with a different scope and rationale in mind. First and foremost, the intention was to highlight the rejection of war "as a means of resolving international disputes", a very attractive statement having a strong (and merely) symbolic and political nature. Secondly, the article in question is aimed at favouring and promoting the international organizations created to ensure peace and justice among Nations: we can say a great deal about the ECCS, the Euratom and the ECC and, now, the Union, but we cannot surely say that their explicit and primary scope is to ensure peace and justice among Nations. All of this, even, regardless of the reciprocity principle which, as per art. 11 of the Italian Constitution, can hardly be considered proven in the context of the Community especially for those matters of which a decision falls upon a majority that can even agree against State interests.

Of course, since, as we know, the intention of the legislators is not the same as that of their predecessors, but that of the current interpreter, it does not come as a surprise that the Italian Constitutional Court, ever since its first chances of delineating the relationship between the national system and Community law, "identified article 11 of the Italian Constitution as the cornerstone. According to this parameter, which has been meaningfully positioned and its consequences on the Italian Constitution measured, the European Communities, now European Union, have been asked to exercise the legislative powers for certain matters in lieu of the Member States and within the limits of the attribution principle".

Perhaps this is how a long constitutional amendment process to solve the "hierarchy" problem has been avoided. However, in my opinion, the relationship issue could have been given an alternative and possibly more compliant and political justification by taking advantage of the experience of the other Member States especially those pertaining to the common law area.

Maybe a reference to art. 10 of the Italian Constitution, and specifically to the well-established *pacta sunt servanda* principle, would have been bolder and more coherent; or maybe even just accepting the fact that following the political decision to delegate to the Union some State prerogatives, within due limits and matters, a subsequent obligation would fall upon the State to comply with the results and the consequences of said delegation keeping the delegate free, as every *dominus* does; or even, due to the political decision; the "source of law" scheme had changed, hence it was not only centred upon and limited to national law or domestic hierarchy, but also finally open to a plurality of legal acts, equal in strength, level and intensity, albeit different in scope and function.

I am well aware of the fact that in covering unfamiliar territories and categories I risk trivialization and error, but I believe the role of the jurist and the comparatist is to try and fit categories to reality and not the other way around. Therefore, I will now try to reason according to this role, first of all by observing, as far as the common law experience is of use, that as the relationship between Member States and the Union is essentially of a political nature, then the delegation of certain matters as Union prerogatives is not a limitation of State power or sovereignty but an exercise of those same powers and that same sovereignty. Furthermore, taking into consideration the peculiar nature of the European Union, more of an "association"[86] of autonomous subjects than an international organization, delegation in its administrative meaning[87] is not as pertinent as some kind of power of attorney (POA) in its "private law" meaning, as in giving power to legally act in one's own name and on one's behalf. This category would perfectly fit the relationship under scrutiny and would explain, in simple and concrete terms, why the State should accept and respect the consequences of conferring to the Union the power to carry out legal acts on its behalf and under its consent.

This "private law" obligation is stronger than the administrative one, since once the POA has been conferred, the "*dominus*" cannot in self-defence ignore or revoke the conferred power, therefore accepting all consequences of the delegate's conducts in advance.

Secondly, if it was indeed the case, the hierarchical "supremacy" of Community law would cease to be a concern: since the norms are enacted and the acts carried out by an entity equal to the State, hence not superior nor suppressing State sovereignty, acting under delegation (or POA), and in the name and on behalf of the State itself, and since norms are also "domestic", there would not be a hierarchy question any more, but rather a primacy as per the object and scope of Community norms. In other words, and recalling again the English system scheme, we would witness a series of norms generated by a political obligation which, in accordance with – rather than against – the validity of domestic law of exclusive State prerogative, are on the same level, compete and enrich the rules, protection and rights of citizens: approximately what we have seen in Common law and Equity, where the latter acts in accordance with the former, although it concretely and always modifies and overlaps with the former, within the due limitations and concessions. Equity follows the law when in reality the judge applies Equity and sets aside the law, similarly Community law follows domestic law, yet in the end the judge applies Community law and sets aside domestic law.

Thus, there is no need to refer to art. 11 of the Italian Constitution to grant hierarchical supremacy to Community norms which, again, are themselves domestic law not hierarchically but "politically" diversified[88].

I am well aware that any objection to this parallelism with the "English model" would bring up the issue of the eventual temporal succession of contrasting if not abolishing norms. In reality, it is a false problem since, first of all, it is an example used at school and secondly, as said and seen previously, the same delegation of legislative power to the Union, evidently has both political and juridical consequences: when the Member State exercise its powers, it proxies the Union and thus accepts all the decisions and consequences; it can reconsider the decision (as no one can bind future legislative power) but any "law" conflicting with Community norms should either be applied outside of the conditions set by the Community norm, or interpreted and applied coherently with Community norms otherwise, at the end of the day, it would call for a political withdrawal by concretely opting out of the Union itself (hence a political choice). On closer inspection I believe the massive case law we have now has never (or at least has not for some time) dealt with the enactment by the Parliament of a law in contrast or even abrogating Community law; on the contrary, the Parliament has used Community law as a loophole to pass the buck of actual harmonization to the interpreters and the judges.

Actually this happens also in other Countries of the Union and to some extent the Italian Constitutional Court has so stated, of course not as openly and perhaps not even as shallowly: I am referring to the "weird" phenomenon of the German Constitutional Court, which claims[89] the possibility of evaluating any contrast between Community norms and constitutional norms, but has never taken the opportunity, not even in the most self-evident situations, to report such a contrast, preferring to take pains to justify the unjustifiable. After all, in addition to the juridical facts and the construction in philosophical terms or the moral and ethical holds, the Constitutional Courts are still fully political bodies that often represent a political group or, in the best case scenario, still have political ties, even just for the appointment mechanism and duration of said appointments[90].

There is still the difficult issue of the "legislative" power held primarily by the European Court of Justice. However, in this case the "delegation" and the transfer of powers to the EU could give rise to a change in the source of law scheme (I am referring to art. 1 of the "Dispositions on law in general"): supposing that this scheme has ever been real, thinking about "the Statutory law" as the only source of law is just a principle statement today. If we want to be more positive towards the positivists, European "norms" as "delegated", as stated before, are by definition also domestic whereas the treaties, which establish the roles and functions of the Court of Justice, are in turn ratified and made domestic and, albeit by broad interpretation, recall the Constitution on the *pacta sunt servanda* principles[91] or, within the meaning of the new art. 177 of the Italian Constitution which, in my opinion, does not change the situation, being confined to a good old and shallow affirmation of principle[92].

Therefore, with the conventional game of magical formulas often used in law, that same source of law scheme would still be abided by, at least formally if not in substance.

This is all to safeguard both the positivistic and juridical approach to the issue, since if we turn towards the political approach and its choices I cannot understand where the problem lies when a State obliges itself to honour the obligation undertaken, as long as the policies do not change. It is quite clear that it is not about a "limitation of sovereignty", but rather about the exercise of that same sovereignty as is clear the fact that the obligation undertaken brings political consequences of significant importance: I am thinking, for example, about the introduction of the single currency and the powers transferred to the European Central Bank and the foreign affairs given to the Union. These are surely not any less relevant than the enactment of law on the width of fishnets or the discussion about the directive on the dimensions of "mechanical contraceptive methods".

Thus, we could paraphrase the English and say that "European law is National law known by another name"[93], except that, as the theory of the fusion applied to the Equity and common law relationship does not work, said theory does not work on the relationship between Community law and law of the Member States either.

This clear evidence would suffice, that is as the relationship between Equity and common law is really a bilateral one, in the issue of Community law there is both a "dualism" between itself and the Member State and a "pluralism" of relationships which end up involving all the actors of this *pièce*. I am not saying we are witnessing a case of the butterfly effect[94] yet undoubtedly as a Community norm is enacted or as a dispute is solved even just apparently in favour of a certain State, the effects of the interrelation between Community law and the law of the Member States are reflected on all the relationships, including those between single Member States.

What I mean to say is that in the case of the European Union we cannot look exclusively at the relationship between Community law and Italian law since Community law will surely influence Italian law and at the same time influences the law of the other Member States, in turn causing an alteration of the relationship between the law of different Member States. Herein we should also consider the reactions created between single Member States. That is why we cannot limit ourselves to looking at the phenomenon only from the internal point of view or considering unilaterally the "fusion of Community law" in the face of the single State.

Once again I refer to the English model and the keen observation of a recent school of thought[95] which States: "normally people suppose that a sound theory of equity must be unitary… however… institutions that come into being unplanned, and grow organically, have no single simple plan. It is no wonder that the Courts of Chancery and common law which came about in that way had no single object, and administered legal rules no single character. A unitary theory of modern equity is inapt. A composite theory, according to which two or more ideas may be necessary to explain aspects of Chancery equity, seems essential".

In my opinion, with due precautions, we can assert something similar about Community law; its relationship with the law of the Member States and their interrelation, as previously stated, cannot be tackled in "fusion" terms, as in a collision between two nuclei which fuse to give birth to a new and heavier nucleus, of which energy is however not simply the sum of the two original nuclei.

By borrowing some notions from physics, albeit with a pinch of salt, in the case of Community law it is better to talk about a "fission": a heavy nucleus which subdivides into 2 lighter nuclei yet stronger in energy which, in turn, interact and generate new subdivisions and new nuclei having new energy, and so on towards an infinite chain reaction.

My experience as a Dean has led me to work with algorithms and flow charts of diverse nature and for diverse purposes: thus, I will try to sum up by borrowing the algebraic language and I apologize for the unavoidable misconceptions in the use of legal concepts which I inevitably must reduce… to their lowest terms.

Fusion of Community law:

(Lgs.M.St.1, Lgs.M.St.n) + S.E.L (Treaties) = Com.Lgs + (Res.L.M.St.1 Res.L.M.St.n) wherein the legal system of Member State 1 and the legal systems of n Member States interact with the Treaties merging with the Community Legal System and "release" nuclei of residual law of exclusive application of Member State 1 and n Member States.

Fission of Community law:

S.E.L (Lgs.M.St.1 Lgs.M.St.n) = Com.Lgs. + (Res.L.M.St.1 Res.L.M.St.n) + (Dom.L.M.St.1 Dom.L.M.St.n) x Com.Lgs. = (Res.L.St.M.1 Res.L.St.M.n) + (Dom.L.St.M.1 Dom.L.M.St.n) + Com.Lgs. wherein EU Treaties (S.E.L) interact with the system of Member State 1 (Lgs.M.St.1) and the systems of n Member States (Lgs.M.St.n), subdividing the latter two nuclei in a heavier nucleus, which is the Community legal system (Com.Lgs.), and in residual nuclei of law pertaining to Member State 1 (Res.L.M.St.1) and to n Member States (Res.L.M.St.n) and to lighter nuclei of domestic law (Dom.L.M.St.1, Dom.L.M.St.n) which, in turn, interact with the Community

Legal System subdividing in even more nuclei triggering an infinite chain reaction.

Hopefully, the following two simple diagrams[96] will better clarify the algebraic formulas pertaining to these phenomena:

*Fusion of Community Law*

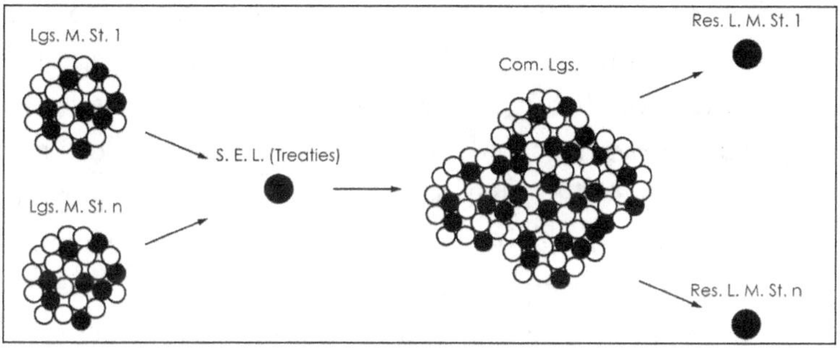


*Fission of Community Law*

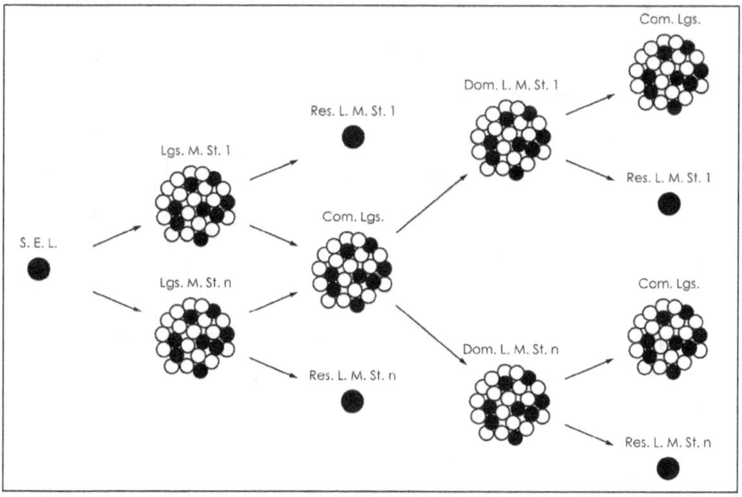

I am well aware that if we had to apply the nuclear fission and fusion theories or more in general physics to law we would be inaccurate.

At the same time, in addition to the algebraic formulas and diagrams, the ideas brought here can be useful, with the due proportions, to simplify and sum up what I have tried to demonstrate up to this point.

The idea or theory of fusion of Community law, and the creation of a superordinate system with regard to the system of "brother" or "relative" States, cannot be applied or deemed valid for all Member States (as they have responded differently to the question), moreover it does not match factual reality, that is the mechanism according to which the interchange between the system of each Member State and Community system works.

Whatever perspective we adopt, the interaction between Community law and law of the Member States cannot be considered static and cannot be justified by trying to fit static categories with an operational reality, which is definitely dynamic.

The point is, and we notice this increasingly every day, that delegation by "brother" States to the Union of the power to enact legislative (and political) acts in their name and on their behalf, be it without waiving their sovereignty and only for limited matters, has triggered a sort of avalanche, a butterfly effect, which no one had imagined possible and no one is capable of explaining, at least amongst Civil law Countries, using the instruments and the categories to which we were accustomed.

As I said, we can find thousands of ways to justify the relationship between the Member State and Community system, but as a matter of fact this relationship is born out of something original and not yet "replicated"[97]. It does not operate in a two-way fashion, but creates a circuit, a flux or a circulation of rules, acts, norms, ideas, policies, interpretations that inevitably end up altering, modifying, integrating, fortifying the law of each Member State and, as a rebound effect, also and again the same Community law, generating an infinite loop or rather a "fission" that continuously generates new energy, new rules, new actions, new protection and new rights.

If this is reality, it is rather useless, as it happens *chez nous*, to continue justifying the relationship between our law and Community law basing our assertions on the hierarchy of the sources and on the "constitutionalization" of Community rules.

It would make more sense and it would be more coherent to accept the fact that the Community experiment has produced a novel situation in the years and we too have to try and reinvent the positive scheme of the source of law maybe by admitting that, as happens in the English experience, today our system cannot curl into a ball but must open, transpose and in turn re-elaborate rules and principles coming from the outside, which are endorsed and operate within the system side by side and integrating with domestic rules and principles.

I do not know whether I have succeeded in demonstrating this last point with flawless legal reasoning; I am nonetheless convinced that the jurist's role is not that of twisting reality to fit the rules and mental categories; on the contrary the jurist should shape and reinvent rules and mental categories according to reality.

Bertrand Russel used to say it was rather unlikely that the universe had learnt from the law of universal gravitation and it was more likely that that theory had been inspired by an observation of the surrounding reality[98].

Continuing to explain the operational reality of Community law and its interaction with the legal systems of the Member States, ignoring the importance and novelty of the mechanism and bending concrete data within the tight space of theories and categories that we are still using, although absolutely abstractly valid, is not "legally" wrong but it recalls the behaviour of that Master of the Rolls[99] who in his will and testament left all his belongings to "fix" the public debt: the bequest was considered very foolish and the testator was considered utterly crazy because, according to the Court, it was as though he had tried to cover the entire central span of Blackfriars bridge with his wig.

# NOTES

[1] In my view, and as my beloved Mentor, Giovanni Criscuoli, has taught me, people's personal stories, albeit so infinitesimal, still influence the system. We will see it here when I discuss the composition of the Courts and, more modestly, it also happened in personal circumstances which inspired and remarkably influenced my approach to this theme.

[2] My specific field of study is comparative "private law" whereas, at least in Italy, European law is traditionally restricted to the 'enclosure' of public law. Frankly, this is something obsolete and not very real given that the points of contact and overlapping between public and private law are multiple and often obvious. Unfortunately, still in Italy, also for banal and trite reasons of castes and university chairs, it almost seems that those who deal with administrative law or constitutional law cannot study family law or contract law, and vice versa, without overstepping their own narrow sphere of competence, as though they were ferocious beasts that cannot be let out of their cages. Thus, even today, as I was saying, European law is considered the prerogative of public law and the 'scientific sector' that encompasses it concentrates on certain essentially public and institutional aspects of the European Union, leaving aside what in English is called the "Substantive law" of the European Union and what the French call 'Droit Matériel', which in Italy 'suffers' the incursions of scholars from various 'areas' (private law, comparative law, private economic law, commercial law, labor law, private international law, and so on). If anyone would like, out of curiosity, to know the cultural "areas" into which Italian "doctrine", not only legal doctrine, has been divided, they can refer to the recent new (2024) classification produced by the Ministry of the University https://www.mur.gov.it/sites/default/files/2024-05/Decreto%20Ministeriale%20n.%20639%20del%2002-05-2024%20-%20Allegato%20A.pdf unfortunately only available in Italian.

[3] Like Alessandro Manzoni's *I Promessi Sposi (The Betrothed)*, this book is addressed to "my twenty-five readers": but far from resembling that magnificent masterpiece, this concise study has no pretensions other than to raise a faint voice of dissonance on a still controversial subject among jurists.

[4] Considering contemporary history, if not for these days, I found *Manuale antiretorico dell'Unione Europea. Da dove viene (e dove va) questa Europa* (Roma 2016) by L. Castellina very enlightening.

[5] Euro-bureaucrats, about whom everyone complains, can be found both amongst economists and professors, the latter often talking about the supremacy of Community law over domestic law and the "subordination" of the State to the "super-power" of the Community and the Union.

[6] "Italy rejects war as an instrument of aggression against the freedom of other peoples and as a means for the settlement of international disputes. Italy agrees, on conditions of equality with other States, to the limitations of sovereignty that may be necessary to a world order ensuring peace and justice among the Nations. Italy promotes and encourages international organisations furthering such ends" (official translation in English by the Senate of the Italian Republic, www.senato.it/documenti/repository/istituzione/costituzio ne_inglese.pdf). The Italian Constitutional Court published a slightly different version of the same art. 11 in English: "Italy shall repudiate war as an instrument of aggression against the freedom of other peoples and as a means of settling international disputes; it shall consent, on conditions of equality with other States, to sovereignty limitations required for a world order that ensures peace and justice among Nations. Italy shall promote and encourage international organizations furthering such ends" (www.cortecostituzionale. it/documenti/download/pdf/The_Constitution_of_the_Italian_Republic. pdf).

As widely known, the most important Italian Courts (as well as Scholars) of our system have authoritatively recalled art. 11 of the Constitution: I am well aware that what is done is done. However, as it will be illustrated later (*see infra*), this reference is very questionable and, as often happens, it looks like there was the intention to make the legislator say something he would never have said. With all due respect to Napoleon…

[7] Inexplicably, the Commission let the Italian Giancarlo Olmi, Vice-Director of the legal department of the Commission itself, express his opinion on the *Simmenthal* case. Indeed, Mr. Olmi was in London in July 1977 (that is, when the case was about to be discussed) to study the English system on site. In his opinion, the system had to be studied and understood due to the ever-increasingly frequent common law matters emerging as a result of the United Kingdom's and Ireland's entry to the Community. On that occasion we happened to study together (at LSE). This is how I got first-hand information and materials from one of the main characters of the *Simmenthal* case. Talking about coincidence…

[8] Or to the ECM as the British, reductively but in foresight, used to say.

[9] of course bearing in mind the difference between "civil law" or French-German inspired systems – as U.S.A. too – and the "pure" English common law system (*see infra*).

[10] Piero Calamandrei used to say: "When politics infiltrates the judiciary through the door, justice gets out of the window". And that "The politicization of judges represents a new danger for justice… the judiciary who switches the seat for the stage of a campaign rally stops being part of the judiciary".

[11] Comparatists have often dealt with these issues and literature on this topic is quite rich: I will only cite an enlightening and clear-cut work that I had the pleasure of reading and that I fully agree with, which was sent to me by Elisabetta Grande, a dear friend and colleague of mine. This work has recently been made available at http://temi.repubblica.it/micromega-online/usa-kavanuagh-alla-corte-suprema-verso-una-dittatura-trump/.

[12] 28 US Code Chapter 121 – Juries; Trial by Jury. The full text can be found in: www.law.cornell.edu/uscode/text/28/part-V/chapter-121.

[13] R. Sacco, *Legal Formants: a Dynamical Approach to Comparative Law*, in The American Journal of Comparative Law, Vol. 39, part. 1 n. 1 (Winter) 1991, pp. 1-34, and part II n. 2 (Spring) 1991, pp. 343-401.

[14] The clearest reference is to the works of A. Watson on the "legal transplant". I suggest at least *Society and Legal Changes*, Temple University Press, 2001 and A. Watson and K. Abou El Fadl, *Fox Hunting, Pheasant Shooting, and Comparative Law*, The American Journal of Comparative Law, Vol. 48, No. 1 (Winter, 2000), pp. 1-37.

[15] Cf. T. Ravà, *Introduzione al diritto della civiltà europea*, Cedam, Padova, 1982.

[16] The chaos theory or "butterfly effect" was founded by the American mathematician Edward Norton Lorenz, who defined "the phenomenon that a small alteration in the State of a dynamical system will cause subsequent States to differ greatly from the States that would have followed without the alteration" – E. N. Lorenz, *The Essence of Chaos*, Taylor & Francis, London, 1995. In a more romantic way as a fan of science-fiction I suggest reading a short story by Ray Bradbury who in 1952 anticipated the "butterfly effect": "*A sound of Thunder*" *(see infra note n. 94).*

[17] The evolutionary line, or rather the parable followed by the Court of Justice, is perfectly described in a concise volume diffused among British students and… those from Palermo, too: R. Kuper, The Politics of the European Court of Justice (London 1998), wherein for example pp.49-50 read as follows: "From 1973 to the mid-eighties, the pattern shifts. The restricted nature of the competences transferred to the Community (the pooling of sovereignties 'albeit in limited fields') began to be eroded, so that no core of State powers was beyond Community reach. This growth of powers 'willed by all actors involved', was often predicated on the 'elastic' Article 235, which became more broadly interpreted – by all parties concerned – than originally intended, when it was merely to allow a legal basis for activities necessary to attain the limited joint objectives of the Treaty already explicitly agreed but where no explicit powers had been granted".

"[T]his wide reading, in which all political institutions partook, meant that it would become virtually impossible to find an activity that could not be brought within the "objectives of the Treaty". A Community without limit to its competences was not what Member

States had signed up to as political oppositionists of all colours have not been slow to point out – nor, indeed, have the supreme and/or constitutional Courts in various Member States. This was not a problem where decisions were made under "the shadow of the veto"; following the introduction of Qualified Majority Voting, however, they are now made "under the shadow of the vote". Issues concerning the legitimacy of the whole construction, buried while Member States had veto control, have surfaced once more. In other words, while Member States might object very strongly to particular Court decisions, the process as a whole was one in which the executive branch of government prospered, together with the judicial, at both Member State and European level. This does not mean there is no conflict between executive and judiciary or between the executive at national level and at European level. Quite the contrary. The latter conflict has often been quite extreme as shown clearly by the behavior of Britain under the Conservatives (and to some extent subsequently under Labour). And the on-going refusal of Member States' Courts to accept supremacy on the Court's terms is a marker that this struggle is by no means over.

Page 51 continues: "A European Court of Justice will of course play an important part in any democratic, decentralised, socially and environmentally aware future construction of Europe. One of its chief roles would be to safeguard and enhance individual and collective rights, rights that derive from a consideration of citizens' needs and humanitarian considerations, not from the abstract needs of the market. The Court bears some of the blame for not having delivered these to date – but only some, given the political climate and lack of vision on which Europe is currently based. These values can only emerge in a genuinely participatory and democratised political process at all levels – local, regional, national and European. And to avoid the Europe that emerges having any fortress characteristics, let it be stressed from the outset that the idea of Europe described above cannot be built nor can it survive in splendid isolation, excluding both at its frontiers and within the poor, the persecuted and the oppressed. A Court dedicated to seeing that people get the rights due to them would need to be much more welcoming to those groups in society who in practice are currently the least likely or able to use it. There is some room even now to use the Court as one weapon in the armoury to further the interests of marginalised groups".

[18] I am not using the term "French-German" to give a political connotation to the unfortunately dominating axis in the European Union. I am using the term to highlight a particular element that is common in the legal systems of all the founding Members. I purposefully did not use the expression "Romano-Germanic" since, with all due respect to R. David's work, the term is based on Roman law as being the common heritage of those States, as opposed to a non-Romanization of English law and common law countries in general. In my humble opinion I have some doubts on the substantiation of this distinctive element. This is not the place for a discussion on this topic but I see the "primacy" of the Statutory law in contrast with other sources as a distinctive element between Civil law and Common law systems: as per definition – Napoleon *docet* and art. 4 of the Code Napoleon is emblematic – the systems which have enacted a codification process in the contemporary era, hence from 1804 onwards, all recognize a single source of law and that is the Statutory law; from a positive law standpoint, there are other "sources" as far as these are explicated by the law itself. On the contrary, in a certain way, and I say so in total awareness of the triviality and over-simplicity of my statements, in Common law systems and especially in the English system there are various sources of law that intermingle and sometimes overlap, which hold however the same strength and full recognition. In simple words we can say (again from that positive law standpoint) that Civil law systems are "single-source" whereas Common law systems are "multi-source".

[19] This in particular is the argument supported by MacKenzie Stuart in his wonderful book *The European Communities and the Rule of Law*, (London 1977). In his study, included in the prestigious *Hamlyn Lectures*, Lord MacKenzie Stuart argued that: "In performing its task

of controlling Community administration – and this, of course, is far from its only duty – the Court of Justice is an administrative Court with a function which corresponds to that of the administrative Courts to be found in all the original members" (p. 14); from another point of view he added (on p. 63) that "The hierarchic structure of the Community law... fits well with the traditions of the eight Member States which have written Constitutions. In so far as one of the duties of the European Court is to determine the compatibility with the treaties of subordinate Community legislation, it is in essence performing the role of a constitutional Court".

[20] Confirmation can be found in the collection of essays on the "*Liber Amicorum*" by Luigi Moccia who also edited the volume *The Making of European Private Law: Why, How, What, Who*, Otto Schmidt / De Gruyter European Law Pub., Munich, 2013.

[21] Not to be contentious, but in my opinion it would also be interesting and enlightening to try conducting a quantitative-qualitative study on the composition of our Parliament (I mean of its members) from the Unification of Italy to these days. If I am not mistaken, some studies of this sort have been conducted by my political scientist colleagues, however not in such a deep and complete manner. It could be an interesting topic for a Master's degree thesis.

[22] A. Miranda, *Il testamento nel diritto inglese. Fondamento e Sistema* (Padova 1995), 83 ss.; on this matter, similarly L.B. Curzon, *English Legal History* (Plymouth 1968), 17; W.S. Holdsworth and C.W. Vickers, *The Law of Succession Testamentary and Intestate* (Oxford 1899), 18; in an accurate argumentation by the leading expert on English law in Italy, G. Criscuoli, *Introduzione allo studio del diritto inglese. Le fonti* (Milano 1994), 104, we read: "The new ecclesiastical jurisdiction extended its jurisdiction in a broad context and, above all, had... very labile boundaries, so much so that these boundaries allowed it, with subtle and jaunty 'spiritual' justifications, to touch progressively broader matters, both civil and criminal, and fundamentally secular".

[23] How stupid these bureaucratic fences which try to enclose knowledge in all these corrals as if it were a fierce beast, are.

[24] Literature on this matter is extensive too. Just to provide a few examples, some titles worth mentioning include: M. Blauberger & S. K. Schmidt, *The European Court of Justice and its political impact*, West European Politics, 2017, 907-918, to which I must add, to give an across-the-Channel view, at least R. Kuper, *The Politics of the European Court of Justice* (London 1998).

[25] Let me please refer to my own study: A. Miranda, *Codificazione e common Law*, in *Atti dell'Accademia delle Scienze, delle Lettere e delle Arti in Palermo* (Palermo 1987), 137-152.

[26] G. Nicolaysen, *Basic Problems of the European Community* (Oxford 1975), 167.

[27] MacKenzie Stuart, *The European Communities and the Rule of Law*, cit., 78.

[28] MacKenzie Stuart, *The European Communities and the Rule of Law*, cit., 78 and 79.

[29] A. Miranda, *Smoke gets in euro eyes. L'uniformazione di norme in materia di buona fede contrattuale in un'analisi euroscettica*, in Vita Not., 1998, 1776.

[30] On this point, for a very informed Italian book on the English legal system, see: G. Criscuoli and M. Serio, *Nuova Introduzione allo studio del diritto inglese. Le Fonti* (Milano 2016), 129 ss.

[31] Data taken from official statistics found in the yearly reports of the judicial activity of the Court of Justice and available at https://curia.europa.eu/jcms/upload/docs/application/pdf/2018-06/ra_jur_2017_it_web.pdf.

[32] The source is of course the official one found on the website where the components of the Court are presented: https://curia.europa.eu/jcms/jcms/Jo2_7026/it. On the issue of the evolution of the Court of Justice see: Y. Dezalay, B.G. Gart (Cur.), *Lawyers and the Construction of Transnational Justice* (Oxon & N.Y. 2012), 217 ss. and specifically A. Vauchez, *The Force of a Weak Field: Law and Lawyers in the Government of Europe*, 219 ss; A. Cohen, *The European Court of Justice in the Emergent European Field of Power: Transnational Judicial Institutions and National Career Path*, 239 ss.

[33] For those of you (very few, I presume) who do not know the

compositions of the two famous cocktails, they are. Negroni: 1/3 gin, 1/3 bitter Campari, 1/3 red vermouth; Bellini: 2/3 prosecco and 1/3 peach juice.

[34] MacKenzie Stuart, *The European Communities*, cit., 1-2.

[35] Case 26/62 (1963) E.C.R. 1, 12. Notably, the decision was delivered in Dutch and the term "nieuwe rechtsorde" was used. It is not superfluous to point out that the case was decided far before the arrival of the Common lawyers.

[36] The sentence in italics is mine.

[37] N. Matteucci, introduction to C.H. McIlwain's *La Rivoluzione Americana*, (Bologna 1965), 26.

[38] C. Martinelli, *Brevi riflessioni sulla rule of Law nella tradizione costituzionale del Regno Unito*, in Diritti Comparati, 2017, https://www.diritticomparati.it/brevi-riflessioni-sulla-rule-law-nella-tradizione-costituzionale-del-regno-unito/.

[39] We cannot forget we are in a Country (i.e. Italy) where "certification" is necessary even for birth and also to demonstrate to be... yet alive (Certificato di Esistenza in Vita or Certificate of Proof of Life). The symbolic norm in art. 1 of our Civil Code says: THE JURIDICAL CAPACITY IS ACQUIRED AT BIRTH. As though we needed some sort of "recognition" by the State to affirm full rights and duties that are acquired for the very fact of being "human". Maybe our norm was put there (and then in the Constitution) to "safeguard" citizens but to me it has always sounded like a minor concession by the legislator/State; unless we consider it redundant like all the mythical constitutional norms based on "rights": very interesting declarations of principle that say everything and their contrary.

[40] MacKenzie Stuart, *The European Communities*, cit. 4

[41] R. Pound, *The Spirit of common Law* (Classic Reprint), (Forgotten Books – Open Access 2017).

[42] Even though I think Lord Nelson can rest easy from the top of his column in Trafalgar Square.

[43] MacKenzie Stuart, *The European Communities*, cit., 3.

[44] The phrase in italics is mine.

[45] MacKenzie Stuart, *The European Communities*, cit., 14. See also: Opinion of Advocate General in Case 9/69 *Sayag v. Ledyc*, 1969, E.C.R., 342.

[46] G. Nicolaysen, *The European Court: its work and its future*, in D. Dagtoglou (Ed.), *Basic Problems of the European Community* (Oxford 1975), 163.

[47] D. Dagtoglou, *European Communities and Constitutional Law*, in C.L.J., 1973, 259.

[48] Cf.: Dagtoglou, *European Communities*, cit., 261.

[49] Dagtoglou, *European Communities*, cit., 259; also the judgment on the European Road Transport Agreement, ECJ, 31-3-1971 c. 22/70, C.M.L.R., 1975, 335.

[50] "Thus far I have assumed that our Parliament, whenever it passes legislation, intends to fulfil its obligations under the Treaty. If the time should come when our Parliament deliberately passes an Act with the intention of repudiating the Treaty or any provision in it intentionally of acting inconsistently with it and says so in express terms then I should have thought that it would be the duty of the Courts to follow the statute of our Parliament" for Lord Denning in *Macarthis Ltd v Smith* [1979] 3 All ER 325, 329c-d. On this issue, and according to what I said, there is a very interesting reconstruction of the line of decisions of the English Courts by L.J. Laws (nomen omen) of the Queen's Bench Division in the Supreme Court of Judicature, in the case *Thoburn v Sunderland City Council* [2002] 3 WLR 247, [2003]QB 151. See also M. S. R. Palmer, *Using Constitutional Realism to Identify the Complete Constitution: Lessons from an Unwritten Constitution* in American Journal of Comparative Law, 2006, 587-636.

[51] MacKenzie Stuart, *The European Communities*, cit., 3. On this issue and for more see the rich *Giudici e giuristi. Il problema del diritto giurisprudenziale fra Otto e Novecento*, in Quaderni Fiorentini, n. 40, Milano, 2011.

[52] MacKenzie Stuart, *The European Communities*, cit., 25-26.

[53] "*if two systems interact with each other for a certain period of time and then are separated, they can no longer be described as two distinct systems, but remain forever and somehow linked, they become a single system*". It is not sure

that this explanation is effectively from P. Dirac but it is easy to find millions of internet pages reporting it under the name of "love formula". Anyway, it seems to me perfectly applicable to the relations between the Member States' legal Systems and the legal system of EU: indeed even after the "Brexit"… "something" British and something of EU or the other Member State can be found in all of them.

[54] MacKenzie himself is particularly sure about it: "… CLASSIC INTERNATIONAL LAW IS AT BEST A DOUBTFUL SOURCE", *The European Communities*, cit., 34

[55] MacKenzie Stuart, *The European Communities*, cit., 26-27.

[56] The problem, as you know, always comes back: as in the most recent decision of the German Court of Cassation on the issue of quantitative easing and the limits of Community law.

[57] I am well aware of the risk I am running in dealing with the problem by jumping from one base to another and mixing different elements, but this is the beauty of comparison: my Mentor, Giovanni Criscuoli, used to say that if it is true that we compare with no definite scope since comparison is a base science then it is also true that comparison can be useful in better comprehending one's own system or verifying the most popular theories, mirroring someone else's theories and maybe indeed grasping some reflections, ideas and solutions, learning to use argumentative techniques different from those we are used to.

[58] Literature on this issue is very broad. For the purposes of this work the first mention due goes to the volume edited by J.C. Goldberg, H.E. Smith and G. Turner, *Equity and the Law. Fusion and Fission*, (Cambridge 2019) (to whom I owe the title of this work and, if you like, also the confirmation of my initial feeling on the issue of the relationship between domestic and Community law). Within the volume in question I would like to highlight the work of G. Turner, *Fusion and Theories of Equity in common Law Systems,* which can easily be found also in its open access version in the Legal Studies Research Paper Series, Paper no. 63/2018, http://dx.doi.org/10.2139/ssrn.3253606.

[59] L. Moccia, *Comparazione Giuridica e Diritto Europeo* (Milano 2005), 213. For one more enlightening and clear-cut work, see: Criscuoli, *Introduzione allo Studio del Diritto Inglese*, cit., particularly the chapter on Equity. But see also the very interesting (and critical) work of A. Burrows, *We Do This At common Law But That In Equity*, in Oxford Journal of Legal Studies, Volume 22, Issue 1, Spring, pages 1-16.

[60] A. Pekelis, *Legal Techniques and Political Ideologies: A Comparative Study*, in Michigan Law Review, 1943, 690-691.

[61] Cf.: H. Finch, *Manual of Chancery Practice: And Prolegomena of Chancery and Equity*, with an Introduction by David E.C. Yale (Cambridge 1965), 191.

[62] MacKenzie Stuart, *The Law of trusts: with special reference to the Trusts (Scotland) Act, 1921, and recent decisions* (Edinburgh 1932).

[63] Ammin. delle Finanze dello Stato v Simmenthal SpA, c. 106/77.

[64] C. Mortati, *Istituzioni di diritto pubblico* (Padova 1991), 299, explains the difference with the abrogation, affirming that disapplication can be considered an instrument that permits "not to apply to a single circumstance or for particular effects an act, which for other circumstances or for other effects is still valid and effective".

[65] I am using "constitutionally" voluntarily in its general meaning, without technical implications.

[66] In relation to this, one of the first comments on the case in question, attributable to F. D. Riccioli, *Preoccupanti contrasti tra Corte comunitaria e Corte costituzionale*, in Foro it., 1978, IV, 206, reads: "The perplexities emerge as the sentence presents again an interpretation of the relationships between Community law and the Italian system that has been copiously contested by our doctrine. In particular, it is to be considered opinable the affirmation of the Court according to which Community norms are superior to national norms, to the point of hindering 'the valid formation of new national legislative acts' if they are not compatible with the former" (par. 17). It again proposes the usual – and more than once contested – pretense of the Court to solve the matter, that of the formal superiority of Community norms over national systems, which goes beyond the competence of the Court and the same Community law, since it

shall be resolved by the *ad quem* system according to the principles and characteristics of the constitutional system concerned. It is true however, that the Court affirms in the following par. 18, that generating and keeping alive national norms that are not compatible with Community law would mean disregarding the international commitments of the State and endangering the base of the Community itself; but this is a problem to be solved in its terms and by not mistaking the role each system concerned has: hence, having cleared the above situation, from a Community law standpoint, an illegitimate act by the State to be sanctioned with the proper procedures; and, from a national law standpoint, the functioning of the internal mechanisms, as and how in existence, to eliminate a law that, albeit still valid in the State, is contradictory to international obligations. Otherwise, once again, as has already happened in the past, we are confusing limits to freedom with limits to the power of the States, since evidently, as things are going for the European integration process, only the former and not the latter are put into discussion" (see A. Tizzano, *Recenti tendenze in tema di competenza a stipulare della CEE*, Foro It., 1973, V, 20 s.; and *Sull'"incostituzionalità" delle leggi italiane incompatibili con i regolamenti comunitari*, Foro It., 1976, I, 2312).

[67] I hereby suggest checking the complete definition of priorité provided by the *Centre National de Ressources Textuelles et Lexicales* https://www.cnrtl.fr/definition/priorité. I have to thank my faculty (sorry… department, I know; but we endangered dean-o-saurs are still fond of our faculty) colleague pr. Antonio Lavieri, professor of French translation studies, who has been a precious source in clarifying the linguistic terms of this matter: this is the beauty of the faculty of Political Sciences, where you can breathe an interdisciplinary air and fruitfully discuss with academics of different fields.

[68] Herein I must thank my faculty colleague Prof. Giulia Adriana Pennisi who teaches English translation and discourse analysis, and was fundamentally important in clarifying linguistic terms and their impact on the juridical aspects of the problem.

[69] Cort. Cost. 5.6.1984 n. 170. See ex multis, A. Pace, *La sentenza Granital, ventitrè anni dopo*, in http://www.associazionedeicostituzio-

nalisti.it/old_sites/sito_AIC_2003-2010/dottrina/ordinamentieuropei/sentenza_granital.html.

[70] With due precautions and taking into consideration we are in a different field, I remind you to recall the Taricco case too, Corte Cost., 31-5-2018, n. 115 and to see the article by F. Guella, *Ci può essere dialogo tra le Corti senza leale cooperazione tra i legislatori? Dal caso Taricco bis al sindacato di costituzionalità "in supplenza" sulla legge penale*, in DPCE online, 1-2018 www.dpceonline.it/index.php/dpceonline/issue/view/34.

[71] Please see: http://www.dpce.it/antonio-la-pergola.html, edited by N. Olivetti Rason, M. Patrono and A. Reposo.

[72] Francovich v. Italy, ECLI:EU:C:1991:428, https://eur-lex.europa.eu/legal-content/EN/ALL/?uri=ecli:ECLI:EU:C:1991:428

[73] The first note by G. Giacalone, *Mancata attuazione di direttive comunitarie e responsabilità dello Stato nei confronti del singolo: un ripensamento della Cassazione?*, in Giust. Civ. 2003, I, 1193; the second is a comment by G. Capilli, *La responsabilità dello Stato per violazione degli obblighi comunitari*, in Alpa, Capilli, Putti, *Casi scelti in tema di responsabilità civile*, Cedam, 2004, 145-160. Other works on the sentence in question: F. Ippolito, *Responsabilità dello stato per violazione del diritto comunitario: osservazioni sulla prassi giurisprudenziale interna*, in Il Diritto del commercio internazionale, 3-4, 2005, (561-577), 574; L. Bairati, "*La responsabilità dello Stato – legislatore la componente culturale e gli impulsi della Corte di giustizia europea nella relativizzazione delle categorie nazionali*", CDCT working paper 6-2012/ European Legal Culture 5, http://www.cdct.it/Pubblicazioni.aspx).

[74] E. Calzolaio, *L'illecito dello Stato per violazione del diritto comunitario, in Lezioni di diritto privato europeo*, edited by G. Alpa, (Padova 2007), 597.

[75] "Any intentional or negligent fact that causes unjust damage to another, obliges the person who has committed the fact to compensate the damage". This principle is close to the conception of the Tort of Negligence as in Donoghue v Stevenson [1932] AC 562.

[76] On this point, there is a curious harmonious convergence with a couple of judgements delivered by English Courts. Please see: James McNaughton *Paper Group Ltd. v. Hicks Anderson* & *Co.*, in NLJ

Reports, 1990, 1311 ss.; *Murphy v. Brentwood* District Council, [1990], 2 All ER 908; but also the very famous *Anns v. Merton London Borough* [1978] AC728. On these cases and about the unreasonableness and the injustice of damages please let me refer to: A. Miranda, *The Negligence's saga: Irragionevolezza ed ingiustizia del danno nel risarcimento delle pure economic losses*, in Riv. Dir. Civ., I, 1992, 387 ss.

[77] Sovereignty belongs to the people and is exercised by the people in the forms and within the limits of the Constitution.

[78] For example, by contesting that the judge had not used the conforming interpretation; and so on and so forth.

[79] As I said before, the required adjustment or better "fine-tuning" of the domestic system with the E.U. directives can be pursued with any instrument and NOT necessarily by a Statute. This means that directives can be implemented by means of an administrative ordinance, an administrative circular, a Court decision, a conforming interpretation by those directly concerned, and so on. What matters is the application of Community law, which is binding, whereas the tools and processes are at the full disposal of the Member States.

[80] Might I also add that neither the revision of Title V of the Italian Constitution nor the new version of art. 177 solve the problem in the intended sense. The statement according to which: "the legislative power is exercised by the State… respecting… the limits deriving from the Community system…" in reality does not add to or take anything from the issue of "independence and sovereignty" of the Italian State and the legislative power exercised by the Parliament which, even though possible, may well decide to use for example art. 50 of the Treaty of the European Union. Saying that legislative power is exercised within the Community limits does not mean imposing an obligation on the Parliament to legislate at all costs and, at most, not to legislate "against", otherwise it would incur in the condemnation of the treaty itself and violation of the political commitments thereby undertaken.

[81] *R. v Secretary of State for Foreign and Commonwealth Affairs ex Rees-Mogg* [1993] EWHC Admin 4 (30 July 1993) URL: http://www.bailii.

org/ew/cases/EWHC/Admin/1993/4.html[1994] QB 552, 1 All ER 457, [1994] 2 WLR 115.

[82] *Miller* & *Anor,* R *(on the application of) v Secretary of State for Exiting the European Union* (Rev 3) [2017] UKSC 5 (24/1/2017) URL: http://www.bailii.org/uk/cases/UKSC/2017/5.html [2017] 1 All ER 593.

[83] Particularly, article J.1.4 (now art.11(2) of the consolidated version) according to which: "Gli Stati membri sostengono attivamente e senza riserve la politica estera e di sicurezza dell'Unione in uno spirito di lealtà e di solidarietà reciproca. Gli Stati membri operano congiuntamente per rafforzare e sviluppare la loro reciproca solidarietà politica. Essi si astengono da qualsiasi azione contraria agli interessi dell'Unione o tale da nuocere alla sua efficacia come elemento di coesione nelle relazioni internazionali. Il Consiglio provvede affinché detti principi siano rispettati". "The Member States shall support the Union's external and security policy actively and unreservedly in a spirit of loyalty and mutual solidarity and shall comply with the Union's action in this area. The Member States shall work together to enhance and develop their mutual political solidarity. They shall refrain from any action which is contrary to the interests of the Union or likely to impair its effectiveness as a cohesive force in international relations. The Council and the High Representative shall ensure compliance with these principles".

[84] *Blackburn v The Attorney General* [1971] 2 All ER 1380, [1971] EWCA Civ 7, [1971] WLR 1037, [1971] 1 WLR 1037, [1971] CMLR 784, URL: http://www.bailii.org/ew/cases/EWCA/Civ/1971/7.html.

[85] For that matter, I do not think neither Monsieur Macron nor Frau Merkel, representing their respective States, have ever assumed a "transfer" or reduction of their power and their sovereignty.

[86] G. Cuniberti, *Conflict of Laws. A Comparative Approach* (Camberley 2017), 335 ss. talks about "*Sister States*" that "*have joined together to form a common entity to which they have transferred parts of their sovereignty. ... By joining the organization, members accept that they have a common destiny. They also agree to share common values, which are typically*

*expressed in documents binding on all members*". Despite the fact it may seem disrespectful, I am more inclined to see the European Union as a polyamorous family where the traditional two-sided matrimonial relationship is substituted by a multiple relationship between different subjects tied to one another by a single ménage.

[87] Hence (trying to give a simple exemplary definition with no other completeness and accuracy pretenses) the attribution of a power of political and/or administrative action from a subject that is a *proprio jure* holder (and so he remains even after delegation), to a subject who is not a right-holder.

[88] Maybe, due to my limits, I have missed something, since I do not understand why we cannot accept a "delegation" of normative powers to the European Union but we accept and tolerate without question a long series of ministerial decrees such as those we have unfortunately witnessed during the Covid epidemic "emergency".

[89] As the Italian Constitutional Court does.

[90] The statement is of course questionable, and I admit my limits in this field. The issue has been better dealt with by other "Authorities": for the Political Philosophy approach I suggest A. Palumbo, *La Polity Reticolare. Analisi e critica della governance come teoria* (Palermo 2013) wherein the author States that "the centralized nation State is progressively replaced by reticular and multilevel political systems where the authority is given to institutions that operate according to specific scopes, have unlimited geographical jurisdiction and accept multiple partakes that tend to overlap".

For a broader and diversified study please see: AA.VV., *Giustizia Costituzionale e Politica*, in Percorsi Costituzionali, nn. 2/3, 2010 (Fondazione Magna Carta) with a wide-ranging op-ed entitled "*Sul mito della Corte costituzionale in-politica*" by Giuseppe de Vergottini and Tommaso Edoardo Frosini, which States: "The decision of wanting to dedicate this volume of Percorsi to the relationship between politics and the Constitutional Court, derives from a theoretical and institutional necessity. The aim is not to clarify the nature and the "political" action of the Court at all costs, on the contrary the aim is to set the function of constitutional justice in the context of the form of government. A theoretical exercise which has been conducted for many years (impossible not to remember the convention on the Italian Constitutional Court and the forms of government held in the 80s) and quite abandoned in the recent years, also because the study of the constitutional judgement of the law has remarkably insisted on the excessively analytical interpretation of the jurisprudence, on the decisional techniques, on the appeals procedure and on the judgements. Hence risking some sort of transformation towards a "constitutional procedure law" in lieu of "constitutional justice", the aim of which may seem to jurisdictionalize to the extreme a body that owns a straightforward legitimation of political nature. Historians such as Francesco Bonini and political scientists such as Patrizia Pederzoli have also conducted interesting research, which have highlighted the political role of the Italian Constitutional Court, either via a reconstruction of the choices on the appointments and the majorities within the body, or via an analysis of the decisions on the policy issue. Jurists, in particular constitutionalists, are instead mostly focused on the technical aspects of the jurisprudence, enclosing themselves in sneaky criticism or, as in the majority of cases, in appreciating it. An example of this is the formula which, for years in doctrine, has moved side by side with the activity and the role of the Court in the system: «the only island of reason in the chaos of opinions»".

[91] It is worth mentioning the very famous, albeit unique and isolated, theory by R. Quadri, *Diritto internazionale pubblico* (Napoli 1968), 59 ss.; also *Introduzione al diritto internazionale pubblico* (Napoli 1963), 37 ss., which in my view is again relevant following the current Community law developments. The thesis focuses on some extremely sharp and coherent arguments we can read in a clear *summa* by G. Tesauro, *Costituzione e norme esterne*, in Dir. Un. Eur., 2, 2009, 201 and 202: "Firstly, a double legislative action of the Parliament to authorize the ratification and to order the execution of the ratified treaty is absolutely unreasonable; even more so if both acts are delivered in the same law. Secondly, the fact that the effect of a domestic law, often prior to entry into force of the treaty, is

rather paradoxical, since it can happen only due to future and uncertain events. Thirdly, this is an unreasonable mechanism of automatic adaptation to the derogations these norms purport on the treaties. The international system is a unitary and organic ensemble; the system and its norms cannot be decomposed automatically giving execution to just some of its norms, without taking into consideration other norms that influence the force of the former.

The arguments opposed to Quadri's theories, were promptly contested by these. The preliminary works were not relevant in his view. The other issue, based on the non-material nature of the *pacta sunt servanda* norm, was also irrelevant according to Quadri, or else overused. All the international norms generate effects on the international system; however, no one stops the States from derogating to the international system in order that the recalled norms permeate domestic law, which are material as in norms on juridical production. The latter enter domestic law so that the former can, in turn, do the same. Now, if everyone agrees that art. 10, subsection 1, consents the automatic permeation independently of customary international norms, how can we justify said automatic permeation independently of the *consuetudo est servanda* norm, which obliges States to abide by customary norms? The same should be true for the treaties and the *pacta sunt servanda* norm.

[92] *See supra* note 80.

[93] The original Court decision States: "*Equity is common Law known by another name*", J.C. Goldberg, H.E. Smith and G. Turner, *Equity and the Law. Fusion and Fission*, cit., 1. I think it is appropriate to say that the relation between Equity and common law can be found in the relation between Statutory law and common law too, of course with all the due precautions.

[94] Taken from the famous quote "A butterfly can flutter its wings over a flower in China and cause a hurricane in the Caribbean"; it probably comes from a wonderful sci-fi short story by R. Bardbury, *A Sound of Thunder*, 1952. In the future, a time machine is used to organize time safaris for tourists. Unfortunately, an excursionist sent to the prehistoric era steps on a butterfly and it causes a chain of

terrible events that changes human history. The chaos theory was later used in Eric Bress' wonderful movie *The Butterfly Effect* (2004).

[95] Goldberg, Smith and Turner, *Equity and the Law. Fusion and Fission*, cit., 15.

[96] The "theoretical" part is under my full responsibility, also and especially for the mistakes that I have surely made while the "transformation" into a diagram is attributable to Arch. Fulvio Miranda, who is also the author of the logo of A.I.D.C. Associazione Italiana di Diritto Comparato (https://www.dirittocomparato.org) and perfectly interpreted my thought (however he remarked that according to his education … physics is not really my *forte*).

[97] As I was saying the European Union is still today an innovative experiment that cannot be ascribed, in my opinion, to any other known international organizations: it is not the Arab League, the ASEAN, the Commonwealth, the UN, the IMF, or the OPEC, it is not the Mercosur, the NATO, the World Bank or the WTO. I am well aware of the fact that the European Union can be considered an international organization, but I challenge anyone to show me that its functioning and its *raison d'être* has something to do with any other international organization.

[98] Cf.: A. Miranda, *Tra moglie e marito non mettere il dito*, in R. Cavalieri and G.F. Colombo (Eds.), *Il massimario. Proverbi annotate di diritto comparato* (Milano 2013), 165 ss.

[99] It concerns the "strange case of Mr. Joseph Jekyll", recalled by A. R. Mellows, *The Law of Succession* (London 1983), 38. See also: A. Miranda, *Il testamento nel diritto inglese. Fondamento e Sistema* (Padova 1995), 274.

# POSTFACE

GIOVANNI BARBIERI

*Cranec Research Fellow - Università Cattolica del Sacro Cuore (Milan)*

This essay can be counted among those rare contributions of a scholarly nature that, with a critical approach, help to better understand the dynamics at play in the surrounding reality and suggest alternatives and solutions to overcome critical situations.

In this sense, "Institutions at Play: Fusion and Fission of European law" sheds a completely new light on the reality of the European Union and its institutions. It does so, clearly, from the perspective of a comparatist jurist with particular expertise in common law, showing how many of the problems that have plagued and still plague the functioning of the EU as a whole depend on a series of typically "supremacist" conceptions of law inherent in civil law systems.

Not being a jurist, I cannot assess the merits of the essay's considerations. Nonetheless, as a political scientist I can calmly argue because of substance, stating that the reasoning on 'fusion and fission' as mechanisms that distinguish the two legal families of common law and civil law is certainly useful in describing some of the "drifts" that have characterised and still characterise the internal life of the EU. Moreover, the essay is built on that dualism to reflect on the functionality of the relationship between EU law and national legal systems.

To articulate my argument, I will recur to the term 'sovereignty' in the next few lines. The reader may be reassured that the concept I want to allude to is that of sovereignty in strict legal terms. Nevertheless, political effects derive from the concept of sovereignty and how it is understood and interpreted by the ruling classes, even more so if the interpretation and understanding of this concept occurs differently among 27 Member States of the same political union.

In this regard, it is worth reflecting on how the Member States have related to the EU order over time. In countries like Italy (and particularly in Italy), the approach to the theme of European integration has always been animated by a strong unionist impetus that has often translated into a not always correct (and I would add dysfunctional) self-limitation of "sovereignty". This attitude often turned into the habit of various bodies of the State to consider EU acts as sources of law hierarchically superior to those identified by constitutional dictates. In this field, as also noted in the essay, this is nothing more than what I would not hesitate to consider 'fiction', since logically (and as centuries of political philosophy have carved in stone) there can be no legal source that has a hierarchy superior to that of a sovereign State. The hierarchical superiority of the EU legal system is nothing more than a political decision, hypothetically also identified by the Constitution and which, like all political decisions has a beginning and can have an end. Considering two legal orders as one subordinate to the other or of equal rank with different complementary competences has important political effects.

From this point of view, the EU is dotted with very different experiences that inevitably produce different results. Considering Italy's strong "compliance" with the EU legal framework, one thinks, for example, of the extreme rigidity of the German legal system which, over the years, has subjected numerous EU acts to the scrutiny of its Constitutional Court. The German Federal Constitutional Court has, over the years, subjected numerous EU acts, mainly falling within the scope of measures relating to the economic-financial and fiscal governance of the Eurozone, to the scrutiny of its Constitutional Court to assess their conformity with the Grundgesetz. Time to time, the Court has constantly reaffirmed that no aspect of German sovereignty in those areas was undermined in the face of the regulatory activity of the EU institutions and that the internal adoption of those new rules was, in fact, the result of a mere political decision. A similar attitude has been maintained by France, which not by chance, together with Germany, has conditioned and, in some way, "directed" the political life and functioning of the EU since the adoption of the Maastricht Treaty.

Ultimately, it can be said that countries such as France and Germany have made their legal systems "coexist" on an equal footing with the EU system by delimiting the areas of competence and without considering their own systems actually subordinate to that of the EU. On the contrary, countries like Italy, marked by a high propensity to take the concept of "the need to regulate" to extremes, have adopted a more supine attitude by signing a sort of blank proxy to the Brussels executive and repealing from time-to-time typical rules of the national legal system that were in conflict with those of the EU legal system. This has been particularly true and evident since, for example, 2012, when the Commission began to draw up increasingly 'intrusive' financial and fiscal governance frameworks with which the Italian executives have complied to the letter. Little did it matter if those schemes then contained objectively problematic elements in terms of ratione materiae effectiveness. This attitude has led, in a Union framework theoretically characterised by a sovereignty shared among the 27, to the emergence of sovereignties that are more sovereign than others and that are better able to protect their own interests within the framework of the same Community order.

Ultimately, it was and is a matter of a different understanding of the concept of sovereignty, which from a legal point of view finds its metaphor in the concepts of fusion and fission effectively introduced by this essay. On the political side it finds its resolution in the "yielding" of certain aspects of the sovereignty of a national legal system in the face of the activity of a supranational legal system. This makes little sense since the supranational legal order arises from an act of political will emanating from the individual actors who give it life and who all remain equally sovereign because they are the only ones, ultimately, able to decide in the State of exception (as, for example, during a pandemic).

The reasoning put forward by pr. Antonello Miranda can also be extended, mutatis mutandis, to the behaviour of the European institutions and, markedly, to the European Commission. The EC, in recent years, has been fascinated and tempted to expand the volume of its competences, probably in the pursuit of the dream of building the "United States of Europe", a theme that has recently re-entered the agendas of some European political movements. Avoiding to enter into an argument about the feasibility of such a project, precisely on the basis of the reasoning presented so far, institutions such as the Commission should change their attitude, i.e. move from the desire to build the "United States of Europe" to the conviction of "doing less and doing it better" (for example, starting from the "regulatory fury" that has defined the rules for the protection of competition on the internal market). This would be an epoch-making change of step, if only for the effectiveness and efficacy of European integration, which would certainly benefit. It is nonetheless true that the Commission's attitude ultimately derives from the political credit given to it by the Member States and that, therefore, such a change in direction can only and exclusively originate from decisions taken at the various national levels (which, hence, remain the true sovereign entities).

To conclude, these few thoughts point out from a polity perspective how the legal insights contained in this essay provide an effective interpretative framework for the dynamics of EU's functioning. Certainly, a different perspective is unlikely to be adopted in civil law systems overnight, i.e. by considering national and EU legal systems as entities that complement each other in parallel (fission) instead of being mutually exclusive in certain areas (fusion). This would be a desirable evolution that would ultimately result from a political realisation and the consequent radical re-interpretation of the nature and purposes of the EU and its legal system, from a conception of hierarchy-subordination to one of coexistence between legal systems (as in common law systems). In other words, taking up the good lessons on the subject that our friends across the Channel left us before they abandoned the project.

## Structures éditoriales du groupe L'Harmattan

**L'Harmattan Italie**
Via degli Artisti, 15
10124 Torino
harmattan.italia@gmail.com

**L'Harmattan Hongrie**
Kossuth l. u. 14-16.
1053 Budapest
harmattan@harmattan.hu

---

**L'Harmattan Sénégal**
10 VDN SICAP AMITIE 3
BP 45034 Dakar-Fann
direction@senharmattan.com

**L'Harmattan Cameroun**
Tsinga/Derrière polyclinique FECAFOOT
BP 11486 Yaoundé
Jacques.koukam@harmattan.fr

**L'Harmattan Burkina Faso**
Villa 281, secteur 23 623, rue 14.32
Ouagadougou
zagbie@outlook.fr

**L'Harmattan Guinée**
Almamya, rue KA 028 OKB Agency
BP 3470 Conakry
harmattanguinee@yahoo.fr

**L'Harmattan RDC**
185, avenue Nyangwe
Commune de Lingwala - Kinshasa
matangilamusadila@yahoo.fr

**L'Harmattan Congo**
219, avenue Nelson Mandela
BP 2874 Brazzaville
deunovmikhael@gmail.com

**L'Harmattan Mali**
Immeuble Mgr Jean Marie Cissé
Aci Hamadallaye
BP 145 Bamako
syllaka@yahoo.fr

**L'Harmattan Togo**
Djidjole - Maison Amela
face EPP BATOME
02 BP 20680 Lomé
didieramela11@gmail.com

**L'Harmattan Côte d'Ivoire**
Résidence Karl - Cité des Arts
Abidjan-Cocody
03 BP 1588 Abidjan
harmattan.ivoire@gmail.com

**L'Harmattan Bénin**
Rue 604, (Immeuble à l'entrée
de la rue UCAO- Cite de Saint-Jean)
Cotonou
stepcorpus@gmail.com

---

## Nos librairies en France

**Librairie internationale**
16, rue des Écoles
75005 Paris
librairie.internationale@harmattan.fr
01 40 46 79 11
www.librairieharmattan.com

**Librairie des savoirs**
21, rue des Écoles
75005 Paris
librairie.sh@harmattan.fr
01 46 34 13 71
www.librairieharmattansh.com

www.ingramcontent.com/pod-product-compliance
Lightning Source LLC
LaVergne TN
LVHW051402061026
849535LV00009B/3314